TO KISS THE
BLARNEY
Stone

KATE CURRY

ISBN 978-1-64300-704-5 (Paperback)
ISBN 978-1-64300-705-2 (Digital)

Covenant Books, Inc.
11661 Hwy 707
Murrells Inlet, SC 29576
www.covenantbooks.com

To Brenden Lee and Emily Grace, the two greatest gifts bestowed upon me in my life. As Brenden is set to graduate from college with a degree in digital journalism and a minor in photography, I applaud him vehemently! He is nothing short of a warrior and will continue to conquer because he had courage. Emily, your love of the arts, talent, and beauty is amazing. Watching you dance lights up my life. You have so much waiting in the wings. You both know I love quotes, and this one is for you both: what lies behind us and what lies before us are tiny matters compared to what lies within us. (Ralph Waldo Emerson)

INTRODUCTION

This memoir has been written over time. Year-to-year time passed, and I wondered how and when things would get easier, but time waits for no one, and it also gets wasted. You take the good with the bad, you struggle, but then you rejoice. I need to thank many people who helped Brenden through the years. Most never treated him like he had "missing pieces." They were in fact those hard-to-find pieces of the puzzle that inserted themselves as missing links; they completed him. I would be remiss if I didn't also thank those who challenged me to seek the resources that would solve or mediate things I could not resolve on my own.

At times, my judgment was clouded by my love for Brenden. I admittedly made many errors through reacting emotionally. However, this journey is far from over. It reminds me of what my mom always said, "Little kids little problems, big kids big problems." The problems were always rearing their ugly head. The solution to those problems is to never give up. You never know your strength until you love unconditionally, until you are a parent.

This story tells about how we navigated the world of autism and square people in a round world. This is my recollection of the events from my memory and experiences. I searched for answers constantly; failing was not an option. As my husband served our country, he could not help me. Once he returned, that war continued, and he still couldn't help me, but he provided for us all. My intuition guided me and kept me focused. My expectations were always high. No stone would be left unturned until Brenden kissed the Blarney Stone.

PREFACE

Soap
Comes in a cardboard square box
Open the package, guess what?
My favorite soap called *Dove*
Shaped Oval in size
Smells rather good
Comes in different colors
Pink and White rather smooth
Greatly used for little ones texture
I know because my new grandchild smells so very good
Just like soap
You get a kiss when he holds the soap
All you have to say is the words "slippery soap."
To Brenden
From Au Pair

The tradition of the Blarney Stone is said to "bestow eloquence on the kisser." "To be able to kiss the stone, you have to dangle yourself from a position, from which if you fell, you would meet your demise." Those who have the blarney could be the lucky ones who have the gift to gab, very talkative people, clever social beings. The eloquence in the art of speaking would be first the ability to express oneself, the fluency to deliver it, and the passion and poise to articulate the words. To bestow is the gift: the gift is to be able to express yourself, to make your needs known, to communicate. Like a door is to a key, autism is a connection to the mind, to reach to teach. Somehow, the honor was not bestowed to my son, deprived to many sons and daughters. All are dangling somewhere waiting to fall, waiting for the failure. But somehow, some way, there is hope, and the joy is within. Our story will tell the truth, as we faced it. It's not about being different. My son knew that already. It also is not about being compared to others. It is about being given a chance. Swinging as you dangle is fine, because we made goals, we made mistakes; we just knew we had to have the Blarney. The silence and frustration we heard would be my son's extinction. To communicate would set things in motion. It was his key to that door. We learned a lot by talking to anyone who could help and had some great teachers along the way. Our message is a strong one, one of struggle but ultimate success. Our story may give you hope. It may comfort you, frighten you. Do not feel alone. I will tell you do not be afraid to dangle yourself. Even though you may be at the end of your rope, you may just kiss the Blarney Stone!

CHAPTER 1

LEARN THE SIGNS

When I was thirty, I got married. I knew my biological clock was ticking. I knew I wanted children. I wanted twelve children. I remember my mom's laughter when I was in elementary school, and I would tell her that I was certain that I would be a social worker because I wanted to help others and that I would marry and live on a farm and have twelve children with twelve horses for them to ride, each and every one of them. We were Irish and Catholic, and of course, this became more immaculate when I married a Curry. How perfect could things have been. We would start our family right away. How hard could this be? One thing we had not counted on was infertility. My endometriosis was suddenly tangling our plans, and the future for having a family would take a new turn. The undertaking of having twelve children was a quandary, but the circumstances would change the endeavor. The beckoning of opening our hearts would be the answer to my prayers, and our families surrounded our optimism with the toddled process of adoption. My family was the backbone behind the journey and adventure of the adoption process. Everyone was all in. In fact, they mobilized a fundraiser to help us fund the cost of the entire adoption process. It was an amazing effort on their part. I will never forget it, ever. The night of the fund-raiser, it was heavily attended, by family and friends. There were raffles of items that my family and friends had either donated or went out of their way to get, like the Lenny Dykstra signed baseball glove. I remember it all, the food the fun and above all the love in that room. I would be a mother soon. It was now just a matter of time.

When Brenden arrived from Korea, he was already six months old. It was one of the happiest days of my life, but I saw the signs the minute he was handed to me. I remember so vividly the day he was put into my arms that he was looking through me, not at me. I had to really support his neck to get him to look at me, and there was never eye contact. In order to carry him, I had to turn him around so he could rest his head on my chest, his head so heavy and bald on the back. Equally important, he made no sound. He didn't cry or seem upset or fussy with us at all, no smiles, no response, no sound. These were the early signs, and I always knew in my heart there was something wrong, but he was all I had wanted; he was my heart.

Shortly thereafter, as a new mom when I brought my baby home, I wanted to give him his first bath. Here I saw other signs. He could not sit up even with support. It was like he could not be bent. He was rigid, in fact. He was already six months old. He should at least be able to sit with support. The bald spot on the back of his head was certainly a conversation piece, and all my family members could say was that he must have laid on his back the whole time he was in Korea. I had been told by the social worker that he had been in the care of one foster mom. I was wondering why she did not hold him, play with him. Did she ever pick him up? So many questions were swirling in my head. I never once thought there could be something wrong with Brenden, only perhaps the care he received while in Korea. Brenden preferred not to be held close. He seemed to enjoy lying on his back and looking at his hand over and over. He would hold his hand up in one place or turn it side to side, all the while just staring for long periods of time. Some of my family would say, "Look, he is waving to us," but I knew this was not the case. I was so happy yet concerned all at the same time. Children at six months do not wave to others. This is a developmental milestone for a twelve-month old. For this reason, as time passed, I realized that I would just have to work with Brenden. Surely he had just been neglected. This had to be why he had so many delays. I thought he could catch up. I was a nurse; I could be the person who could help him the most.

At his first doctor's visit, there was no discussion about developmental delays, just the trauma of getting his blood work done. We had to make sure to rule out the possibility of HIV, hepatitis, and tuberculosis. Even though Brenden had medical care while in Korea, the doctor kept saying that we could not trust the blood work or any of the medical papers that were sent with him. So to protect him, we agreed, but they were unable to find a vein and thought he could be a little dehydrated from the trip. They had to draw the blood from his jugular vein in his neck. I had to leave the room while my husband stayed to help hold him while the doctor took the sample. It was breaking my heart. I wanted to stop the doctor, but eventually, everything was over and the sample obtained.

I often thought about that appointment and the fact that the doctor saw none of the developmental delays that I had seen almost immediately. He seemed so very interested in his medical history of his six months in Korea. I showed him all the papers that we had been given, and he kept saying that the information was unreliable. Without question, he did not see what I was seeing. He never even asked any questions. All he wanted was the blood sample, and we all know autism is not diagnosed in a blood test. Autism was never a thought in the doctor's mind nor in mine, but there were signs. If I only knew the signs . . .

During this time, I was on family medical leave from my job, so I knew I had six special weeks to devote myself to my son. I also had a video camera that my cousin Maryanne had lent me to capture the happy moments as my son and I grew to know each other. Now when I watch these tapes, I can really see what I was blinded by at the time, all because I didn't know what I was looking for. I was a first-time mom, and I had a child who seemed to need so much. I always heard that every child develops at their own speed, and people were constantly telling me this. Besides, I also knew how important the six weeks would be for us to bond with one another.

It seemed like forever, but eventually, Brenden could sit up without support. I refused to have him in the playpen or to lie in the crib for that matter. Any upright position was how I liked to see him. I also liked to keep him focused and stimulated with all kinds of toys or rattles, anything that made sound and he would respond to. More importantly, the outstanding issue was that I continued to see Brenden's total lack of verbal and nonverbal responses. At times, he would smile, not back at me, mostly at objects he would target in on around the room. He rarely made eye contact with anyone. It always reminded me of the first day with him when he looked at his hand. When he heard a sound, he didn't respond to it, and he never turned his head when I called his name. After six weeks, he should have responded to his name, but it was as if he didn't hear me or the world around him at all.

Any social game like peekaboo that I tried to involve him in was met with no response. Brenden did not acknowledge sound. In fact, he made no sound. He rarely cried. He would soon be eight months old, and then time ticked on. He was now suddenly twelve months old. I told the doctor that I did not think he could hear me. There were no words, especially the ones a mother and father wait to hear, like *Mama* and *Dada*. There was also no patty cake or clapping hands and yelling hoorays! Brenden did not notice the people in the world around him. There was no need for the word *no*. He never explored on his own. When he played, he preferred one toy to all the others. Clearly, his favorite toy was a *Sesame Street* train. He would push that train around and around for hours. I had another surgery at this time for my ongoing problematic female issues, and my sister was at the house to help take care of Brenden. I could hear them downstairs playing, and my sister would keep saying, "Choo-choo!" as he pushed the train. While I lay upstairs, even the effect of the pain medications could not block my awareness of the fact that Brenden could not repeat this sound of the train. He never even tried. I prayed that we would soon hear sounds from him, but no one was aware of the signs, and those precious early years would pass by without answers.

According to the CDC,

By the end of seven months, many children are able to

- turn head when name is called,
- smile back at another person,
- respond to sound with sound, or

- enjoy social play (such as peek-a-boo).
- By the end of one year or twelve months, many children are able to
- use simple gestures (waving bye-bye),
- make sounds such as *Ma* and *Da*,
- imitate actions in their play (clap when you clap), or
- respond when told no.
- By the end of one and a half years (eighteen months), many children are able to
- do simple pretend play (talk on a toy phone),
- point to interesting objects,
- look at an object when you point to it and tell them to "Look!" or
- use several single words unprompted.

CHAPTER 2

CHILD FIND EARLY INTERVENTION

Brenden turned two in October, and a few months later, it was suddenly Easter. He was walking when he was supposed to be running. His motor skills were lagging behind; his muscle tone was very weak. He seemed much more interested in picking things up off the ground and examining them, forever! My mom would come and take him for walks while I was at work. She would tell me that she loved what he found on the ground. She would even paint things he would find and keep them at her apartment. One, she said, was just some branches, but to her, it looked like a bird. She painted it pink. Sure there are pink birds. I was thinking, *Okay, well, this is certainly of no concern, and my mom seemed to think they had so much fun together!* Soon, Brenden started to show a particular interest in paper. He also would take my wooden spoons and decorate them. Inexplicably, I guess some people might say that he was creative, but I felt so differently about these odd behaviors.

His play was all so casual; for example, he would take an electrical cord and wrap it around different objects so that he could pull them around like a train. I can also recall that while playing with his Thomas the Tank trains, he would become so overly focused on building a bridge, and of course, it had to be perfect. Lining things up, all the time, no matter what it was, always in the same order. I worried about this, and then reality would collide into my thinking. I wondered if he would ever potty train. He was soon to be three.

School was coming quickly. But as we know, life moves on. Time was again ticking away. We were moving to Maryland. We wanted another child, and we decided we were going to adopt again. In all the change, I never once thought about Child Find or early intervention services offered through the school districts for Brenden. I had no knowledge that the schools were mandated to locate children who may be at risk from birth to age twenty-one. I was still hearing what I thought I needed to hear. Every child is different and develops at their own pace. But I knew I felt differently. My intuition told me there was something wrong, but what?

Before we moved, I can clearly remember Brenden was sitting facing away from me. I entered the room and called his name. He did not respond. I called his name again, and he still did not turn to the sound of my voice. I took him to the doctor with my concerns. The doctor listened this time. The doctor then picked up a book and dropped it on the floor. Brenden had no reaction. The doctor looked at me. His face was as blank as a fresh piece of white paper. He recommended that I have his hearing checked. I didn't know how this could possibly be. Seriously, could he be deaf? I made the appointment immediately, never thinking twice about it. I wanted to help him. This was a start. We went to the children's hospital, and I was overpowered with emotions the entire day. There were so many sick children there. I thought how lucky we would be if Brenden only couldn't hear! Some of these kids were in wheelchairs, some had feeding tubes and tracheostomy tubes, and we could walk in on our own. I was certain in the fact that even if there was a problem with his hearing, it would never be as severe as what we saw all around us. I felt just a little bit relieved, but in time, this, too, would pass.

The audiogram could not be performed because Brenden was too young. The hearing test they gave him was in a soundproof room, and there was a bear with cymbals. The bear crashed the cymbals together, and the tester simply watched his reaction from the noise in the room. I watched as well, and I could tell he could hear. I also noticed that he was covering his ears as if there was pain. Those sensory responses were basically overlooked by the tester, but I was so grateful his hearing test came back reported as normal. So as my physician reported the wonderful news, no further thought or investigation into my concerns about Brenden not meeting his developmental milestones was discussed. We continued to act like everything was normal. I went to work, then came home to a long night. My husband worked night shift, so I had to come to the reality of either quitting my job or cutting back. My boss was very accommodating, but I knew where my heart was, and it was with Brenden.

Staying home, I noticed more and more that things were not progressing in regards to Brenden's development. He spoke very little and also showed no emotion. I decided to use picture cards with the words to attempt to get him to speak. In fact, even if I had the (word) *ball*, I would also get a ball so he could touch the object and hear me say the words. He would watch, but never did he utter the words. In years to come, I would be amazed at his vocabulary word base. Even though he would not say the word, he would point to it. In retrospect, I asked a speech therapist at Dupont if I did him harm by allowing him to point and not say the words. She told me if I hadn't done that, he probably would not be talking at all. Well, one point for me, but I was meandering around as if I was on a different planet. I was unsettled. I was searching for something any vindication to my gut telling me: there was something wrong.

After our move to Maryland, Brenden was turning three; but now, along with our new home, we also adopted our daughter, a beautiful healthy girl named Emily. She helped me see a lot of things. Emily was hitting every milestone developmentally. I started to notice that more and more, a lot was wrong with Brenden. At ten months, she was walking, at one and a half years talking. Brenden was now four years old and still in pull-ups. I thought if I could just get him into school, everything would be just fine. Emily continued to show me the signs. She was a child that cried a lot, but she also needed to be held just as much, and I thought her needs were so minimal compared to Brenden's. He had no interest in playing with other children, and if I took him to play, he would sit alone and play alone as well. He did not notice the other children. He did not play make-believe. He seemed to be unable to relate to anything, except for the things that absorbed him. Emily, on the other hand, arrived in the middle of all this turmoil and confusion. Be that as it may, she was such a joy to me, a ray of sunshine on my shoulder every day. She would in later years become my greatest remedy. A flashback comes to mind of something she typed up on the computer about autism. She said, "I have a brother. His name is Brenden. He has autism. He gets frustrated with homework. He has stress toys to help him feel relaxed." Emily knew I needed her, and that feeling was mutual. I could tell you about her, but that's another place and time. Some people come into your life for a reason, even little people.

Brenden was now four years old. He couldn't follow two-step directions, get dressed, brush his teeth, or comb his hair. All his activities of daily living were being done by me. He showed no diligence to learning any of it. He started to actually hate having hair on his head. He always wanted a buzz cut; the less hair, the better. He was in his own little world. He was happy yet desolate. Sensory issues presented often. I couldn't have any perfume on or hair spray. He could only eat certain foods, and he would smell it first. He also could identify a piece of clothing and whom it belonged to by smelling it first. A prominent memory was when my cousin Maryanne had sent some clothes down to me, and he picked it up smelled it and said, "Mare, mare." Wait, what about school? I was sure it was the answer. I needed the answer. Who had the answer?

Needless to say, we were not going to pre-K on time. We were not going to be even potty trained on time. This was another hurdle or challenge. Brenden did not seem to be able to do this even at age four. I remember vividly as I was trying to care for Emily and then trying to put Brenden in the bathroom to sit and try . . . Then he would run out and pee on the kitchen floor. Even if I sat with him in the bathroom, he wanted off. Nothing worked. I even had him sit on his own potty when I was in the basement trying to do laundry . . . He would stay there and talk, in his unintelligible way. I loved him so. What could be wrong?

According to the CDC

By the end of two years (twenty-four months), many children are able to

- use two-to-three-word phrases,
- follow simple instructions,
- become more interested in other children, or
- point to an object or picture if named.
- By the end of three years (thirty-six months), many children are able to
- show affection for playmates,
- use four-to-five-word sentences,
- imitate adults and playmates (run when other children run), or
- play make believe with dolls, animals, and people ("feed" a teddy bear).
- By the end of four years (forty-eight months), many children are able to
- use five-to-six-word sentences,
- follow three-step commands ("Get dressed, comb your hair, and wash your face."), or
- cooperate with other children.

According to the Maryland Department of Education early learning office, these are some things that a four-year-old should be able to do at age four, before heading off to pre-K.

- Know how to ask an adult for help
- Recognize his or her first name in print
- Recognize a favorite book by the cover and ask that it be read out loud
- Be curious about letters, words, numbers, and counting
- Repeating parts of rhymes or some words from a familiar song

- Following basic two-to-three-step directions, such as "Get your coat, put it on, and stand by the door."
- Following basic rules at home, like putting away toys

Reality check Brenden could not do any of this, but it school, right? I mean that's why you send your child to school, to learn. He would catch up. Surely, school would be the place to see these issues and work on them. The guidelines to be entered into the program were that the child be four years old by September 30 and be toilet trained. They also stated that the child needed to come from an economically disadvantaged background (be eligible for free or reduced meals) or that no permanent address was available or homeless. So I thought, *Well, we don't meet any of those requirements.* But they also wrote that a child who exhibits a lack of readiness in early learning or social development could be enrolled. Well, there it was. Surely, this would be a way to start him on his way to catching up. I thought, *All I have to do is work on the potty training, and we would be late, but on our way!* Trust me, I had no idea what events were about to unfold. Potty training would be a snap compared to taking on a school district. Potty training is just all about waiting and trying to keep that schedule for the child. I would sit him in the bathroom just about every two hours to try and go. Funny, as I mentioned earlier, I remember having so much wash one day I put a potty right in the piles of laundry. He just sat there with his books, and I did laundry. He had the best success when I would throw cheerios in the toilet. He found that so interesting. But, honestly, it was when I had my cousin's son David take him in and show him how to pee in the toilet that really pushed him to try. As always, too much verbal language, much easier to show him what he needed to do. Simple but effective.

We did finally get to pre-K after half a school year had passed, but we were there! I was so nervous to leave him. He had never been away from me. Brenden seemed to watch me leave, but he didn't cry, yet. As I drove home, he was constantly on my mind. I really could do nothing more than worry. It was like an out-of-the-body experience. I recall the wind being warm on my face, as I drove frozen in my seat. Time passed, and honestly, this was a half-day program, so I just thought, *Well, I didn't get a phone call, so things should be going okay.* This could not be further from the truth. When I arrived for pickup, I saw him coming down the hallway holding the aide's hand. He was screaming and crying. The aide looked at me and reassured me he is "fine." I just picked him up and hugged him, in that crowded hallway with everyone looking at us. Surely, they must have been curious. I must say that we got through pre-K, but it was a blur. Brenden and I do not recall much about it, except for a few things. First, we met some great lifelong friends, both of us. The other moms were neighbors and friends who would be my rock, the people I could count on. We did lunches together at Applebee's, and I could escape in conversation. They would also look after Brenden when I wasn't in the classroom, and they were there to help out. They never judged or looked away. Their kids were kind and helpful. Yes, that is what we remember and will never forget. Maybe that is because on the horizon was the kindergarten year, and we still are not sure how we got through it . . .

Brenden's Landscape: The Early Years

I knew I was a different child. I knew from the moment I realized that I was adopted, I was a different child.

I do recall crying on the first day of pre-K because I was away from my mom for the first time.

I had only one friend in kindergarten, Tanner.

I had a few friends.

I also recall my many years with my cousin David, who lived down the street from me in Maryland.

CHAPTER 3

AN APPROPRIATE EDUCATION

There were a lot of bad memories from kindergarten, Brenden recalled. "I was sent to the office and had to sit with Mrs. Wallace. I felt upset, and I did not like that." The procedure for pickup at this school was you waited in the hallway until they brought the children out. So I was there first, of course, because every day I dropped him off, I worried and worried about how he was doing. I see the principal come out of a side door to the office, and then I see my son holding her hand as she apparently was returning him to class. Another mom stated, "Did you see that?" Everyone in that hallway was staring at me, then at Brenden. I didn't even know what to say or do, so after he came to the line, I walked right back down to the classroom, for some kind of explanation of why my son was in the office. I mean, did they do that on purpose? Was I just to pick Brenden up and go home? The teacher explained that he had to be removed from the classroom. She seemed nervous, unsure of what to say to me. I tried to explain, in the middle of dismissal, that, as a parent, seeing your child escorted out of the office was not exactly a feel good moment. This started an avalanche of notes coming home to tell me about Brenden's daily focus, or lack thereof. For example, and these are exact word-for-word notes I received.

March 19, 2002

Brenden had some difficulty at math. Mrs. Short sat with him and helped him, but he deliberately broke two crayons so he had to finish his graph with a pencil.

April 17, 2002

Brenden did well on a following directions paper. He was a little frustrated in the computer lab, but I helped him, and he did a very good job!

April 18, 2002

Brenden was frustrated in math today. He refused to do his work counting pennies and nickels to pretend to go shopping, so he had to come back and do it at his free choice time. He sat next to me and did much better.

April 22, 2002

Brenden had a difficult time at writing today. Twice he scribbled all over his paper and crumpled it up. Then he broke two crayons and had to color with a pencil again. He kept disturbing the other children, so he sat by himself, then had to stay and finish his work during his free choice time.

April 30, 2002

Brenden did a great job in math. He sat by the fish tank, and I worked with him one-on-one while doing the group lesson.

This is just an example of what I read on a daily basis. There were many assignments that were given that involved following directions. Most often, they would be multistep directions and most often verbally read to the class, as they would not be able to read that on their own. I started to notice how much help he needed and that with that support he could complete the work. Often, he would break his pencil points or crayons in frustration. This always resulted in a negative reinforcement. In other words, he was removed from something because of his behavior; hence, he got out of doing it. This increases the chances that it will happen again. That was not helping. Brenden started to notice that when he broke a crayon, he was told he had to use a pencil. Then because his work was not all in crayon, it did not get displayed with the classwork that was hung outside the room. Imagine that he would notice that. Yes, he, indeed, did notice that. What I wished was that he would have been given a break, then supported to complete the work at a later time. What I wished for was that he could be understood. Things were just amiss. Brenden stood out like a sore thumb, like exhibit A.

I decided that I would go to kindergarten with him. I watched him easily become frustrated with verbal directions and other noises in the room. If other children were writing on the floor, he would get up and stomp on their papers. At other times, when he would be writing, he became frustrated, which was most of the time. He would start scribbling on his or another child's paper. He used no words. He would scream or grunt in an attempt to tell someone to help. Usually, I would just take him out of the classroom to comfort him. Sometimes, this worked. At other times, I would take him home, but he would bang his head on the glass window of the car. Once home, it was back to his own little world. He would get his faithful Thomas the Tank trains and watch them go around the track, over and over. Then he would make them go in reverse. It seemed to calm him. The train is on the track. *Click clack.* Do I have to keep sending him back?

It wasn't long until the speech screening came along. Even though Brenden did have some words now, he rarely used them. I remember when I registered him for pre-K, the office secretary asked me if he needed speech. I assumed she thought because he was Asian, he didn't speak English. But in hindsight, the whole time we were in the office, he didn't utter a sound, and now I am sure that she was referring to his lack of language and not his ethnicity. Either way, the speech screening, followed by the psychological assessment, landed me and Brenden into the world of special education.

The speech screen was completed. Brenden did not pass the three language subtests. He had difficulty with vocabulary and knowledge of language concepts. The only good news I was told was "he seems very bright." The teacher reported that Brenden worked one-on-one with a parent volunteer four days a week. He often needed help getting started on his work and had difficulty completing it. He often needed redirection during his work periods and could easily become discouraged. She added that he had trouble interacting with peers and was grabbing things from them instead of asking. She went on to describe that he could not follow directions and had difficulty expressing himself verbally. It was determined that he would need a full speech and language evaluation to assess his articulation, and receptive and expressive language skills. Along with that, he would have a full educational evaluation to assess his readiness skills in the area of fine motor, matching and counting, along with gross motor. Finally, a psychological evaluation to determine his ability and if processing deficits existed.

First and foremost, no one can prepare you for the moment that they announce at a meeting that your child may have a learning disability and may be eligible for special education. What actually makes it worse in our case was that the school did not really identify what type of disability. I was thinking, *Well, learning disability, but it seems to be more complicated than that.* Complicated doesn't even begin to explain what the next three years would be.

In January of 2002, I attended the IEP (Individual Education Plan) meeting to discuss the results of the educational evaluation. Nervous doesn't even begin to describe my emotional state. I was alone. I thought I was ready to hear how they would help Brenden. I was told the following:

His fine motor skills and writing were seven months delayed.

Fine motor skills were thirteen months delayed.

He had difficulty with fine motor skills (lacing and copying designs).

His gross motor skills were seven months delayed.

He had difficulty with catching and throwing objects such as a bean bag.

His speech was difficult to understand especially in conversational speech.

The clinical evaluation of language found his language skills were over a year below expected for his age.

Weaknesses in receptive and expressive language skills.

His score on the Peabody Picture Vocabulary test were above normal.

It was noted that he does not make eye contact and use turn-taking skills.

The psychological evaluation showed Brenden had an IQ of eighty-four, placing him in the low average range.

A significant twenty-eight-point difference was found between his verbal skills and performance skills, indicating his lack of verbal skills was influencing his achievement. It was noted when a visual cue was used he performed better.

His visual motor coordination was very weak in the area of drawing and copying.

So there it was. Then the "team" stated that due to his fine motor skills and language skills being significantly below his ability, special education services were warranted. I was staring at the reports. I was looking around the room. I was starting to cry. I was waiting for the empathy, the reassurance the kind soul to reach out and tell me not to worry! No one did that. I was the one who was languishing. This was a routine day for the staff. I asked myself, *What kind of team is this? Am I a member of this team too?* Apprehensively, I sat in the room. Sadly, I would soon find out there is *no I in team, and the I is me!* Ignorance to the system has now made me vulnerable, and I had to figure this out quickly. Brenden needed me to be there, and I needed to show up.

The IEP was then proposed, *Was I really hearing this, or was this a dream? Why is my son in this circumstance? Am I to blame?* These

were the following goals and objectives read to me. It could not have
been a more exhausting experience.

Speech: The student will improve articulation by mastering 100
percent of the following objectives:

Target sounds were *l, v, th, s* blends. The sounds will be pro-
duced in isolation, syllables, words, sentences, and conversation. The
student will improve auditory attention, receptive vocabulary, receptive morphology/syntax, auditory memory, semantic relationships by
mastering 100 percent of the following objectives. Note to self, I am
now so confused that I am not even sure any of this can be done?
A hundred percent! I cannot even understand what this all means,
and Brenden has to master this? Okay, I will continue to listen, to
appear like I am in total agreement with this person who, *I understand, wants to help my son communicate.*

Brenden's Landscape

*I vividly remember this with Mrs. Lantz. I can remember I would
be pulled from class two or three days a week to work on these phonetic
sounds. I can remember saying, "I frew the ball," instead of "I threw the
ball." Some days were with two to three kids. Some were just one-on-one.*

He will maintain eye contact with the speaker and demonstrate
increased comprehension of nouns, verbs, adjectives, adverbs, and
prepositions.

Brenden's Landscape

*I didn't fully grasp the eye contact skill until I don't remember when,
but maybe the reason was how I was getting interested in girls. Or maybe
it was because I followed what the normal people would do.*

He will demonstrate increased comprehension of basic concepts
of space, position, quantity, quality, time. She tells me he has difficulty with time. I can relate as I am having difficulty at this moment.
Should I be making eye contact? She continues, saying he will be able
to follow single-step commands. He will be able to recall significant
facts in three-sentence paragraphs and fill in the missing parts of

28

phrases, and, in finality, will use turn taking in conversation. Sure, I think that would be nice to have a chance to talk, to be in a conversation, to say something profound. But I cannot utter a sound. She continues. He will improve expressive vocabulary, morphology/ syntax, critical thinking skills, and conversational skills by mastering 100 percent of the following objectives. He will formulate a complete grammatically correct sentence using one word. Wait, a sentence only has one word? I thought that was just a word. Dear Lord, I knew he was in trouble. How could I have let things get this bad? What kind of parent am I? She talks about expressing differences and similarities about nouns and identifying objects with a definition. Express a word within a category, and explain absurd, illogical, or humorous statements/pictures. Things do not seem like they will be funny. In fact, I can see my frustration growing at my own inability to get a grip right now! The meeting moves forward.

Fine motor: The student will improve fine motor skills by mastering 100 percent of the following objectives:

Brenden's Landscape

I remember the big fat rubber grips teachers would put on my pencil. I thought I got that because I was special. I remember them being blue.

Lacing cards independently; manipulate scissors to cut on a line; copy shapes that include circles, squares, rectangles, triangle; and my favorite, color within the lines. Oh well, I can picture this. I can even see the light here. This should be easy compared to all the other work to be done. I am overwrought. At this point, I actually think I could go running and screaming from the room. I could now see how overwhelmed Brenden has been feeling, trying to get through his day. I knew this would only escalate an already high-stress atmosphere that honestly I did not understand. How would he survive this? I blamed myself, but the love I felt for him was so evident in my mind. I knew that in this moment I had to educate myself. This is not going well. I do not understand the process. What is wrong with him? My ignorance to all of those obvious delays in his speech, motor, and social skills were now in the forefront; the elephant was in the room.

Brenden's Landscape

From first to third grade

I worked with special education teacher Mrs. Rebecca Peacock and Cindy Hamilton, a paraprofessional. I remember having Mrs. Hamilton writing for me. I remember having her and I split writing. I remember her sitting next to me in the front row of the classroom.

I can recall thinking to myself that I would be doing my schoolwork in a jail cell in a prison uniform. I thought I had nothing to work for back then. I remember the smile chart. It had a subject and had two spots. One for the beginning of the period and the end of the period.

I knew I was a good kid. I didn't know how to do it.

CHAPTER 4

THE OUTSIDE EVALUATION

So what do you do after hearing this kind of information for the very first time, about the one true thing in your life that is counting on you to make things better? He was five years old. This was happening in a very accelerated manner, yet time was standing still. But I thought, what does he need most? He needs to be able to express himself. That was crystal clear. His overall language scores were over a year delayed. His verbal skills were deficient at times based on the demand. So this is what you do: you do nothing in that meeting, and you go home to reflect unless you are in complete agreement with what you are being told will help your child. While I was reading, I'm thinking as I read and reread, what is his biggest weakness? His delays in communication are completely exposed, and even though he will receive thirty minutes three times a week, will that be enough? Wow, that did seem like a lot of time out of class, but somehow, it was necessary. He had so many goals to work on. I had to read them again and again and envision a plan of my own.

The student will improve articulation by mastering 100 percent of the following objectives:

- will produce target sounds in isolation, syllables, words, sentences, and conversation. The sounds were *l, v, th, s* blends (this is not a concern and not a worry for me).

The student will improve auditory attention, receptive vocabulary, receptive morphology/syntax, auditory discrimination, auditory memory, semantic relationships by mastering 100 percent of the following objectives:

- will maintain eye contact with the speaker in a small group discussion
- will demonstrate increased comprehension of nouns, verbs, adjectives, adverbs, and prepositions
- will demonstrate increased comprehension of basic concepts of space/position, quantity, quality, and time
- will be able to follow single-step commands.
- will be able to recall significant facts in three-sentence paragraphs
- will demonstrate the ability to fill in missing parts of phrases and sentences
- (Okay, here I am thinking, yes, follow commands good, recall facts good, fill in missing parts, excellent. Eye contact, not so important. Comprehension maybe that should not be a current concern . . .)
- The student will improve expressive vocabulary, morphology/syntax, critical thinking skills, and conversational skills by mastering 100 percent of the following objectives.
- will formulate a complete grammatically correct sentence using *one word*
- will express characteristics of a given noun
- will express similarities among nouns and differences among nouns
- will, when presented with a definition, identify the object described
- will express words within a category
- will explain absurd, illogical, or humorous statement/pictures
- will use turn-taking skills in conversation

(Now how is forming a sentence using one word going to help him express himself? This concerns me. Explaining humorous statements, should this be in this goal?)

So here is what I looked at, in print from the IEP meeting where I only participated as a statue. As I sat at home reading the information, it started to sink in. When you look at the goals in this way, you can digest them. In the meeting, it was all too swift, catapulting me into the rabbit hole, like Alice in Wonderland. But I had to use logic on this journey, because this was real, not a fantasy. There was so very much I didn't know about the educational system, and my new goal was to get up to speed and search for the answers. I had to educate myself on my son's rights. But I also knew I had a responsibility to remedy some things on my own. I also thought the school day has only about six hours in it. There is so much you can and probably should do on your own in conjunction with the Individual Education Plan. When I was at work, I talked with my friends about what I should do. One told me that she had just had a psychological assessment on her son and would highly recommend the doctor to me. So I called and made that appointment, but it would be three months from now. I was so pressured to get this right. What was this spell I was under? I was walking around with the future looming and the present time so confusing. Consequently for Brenden, he had the frustration of enduring the world I told him to fit into. The questions were mounting while the answers were nowhere to be found. I guess you could say I was scatterbrained, one big space cadet!

In the meantime, I did sign that IEP, full well knowing that any help was better than no help at all. Then in March when Brenden was five years and four months old, we were full in and getting that outside evaluation. I guess I didn't know what to expect, but I was grateful she allowed me to stay while testing. While she interviewed me, she gave Brenden toys to play with. In the report, she noted that although he was interested in the toys, he repeatedly sought my attention, asking for my help. I really was unaware of that at the time, and honestly, I just redirected him back to independent play. She also stated that each time I asked him to play with the toys, his activity level rose. She also noted that his attention was brief in nature along with random in nature. As I think back on that moment in time, I wonder if she thought at all that he may just be anxious and nervous. I mean he didn't know why we were there. He was in a unfamiliar place, and to be quite frank, I think any child would seek out their parent for emotional support. Even during the testing part of the evaluation, when he was asked to do something, he would first seek me out. I do remember reassuring him to try it first. I do not remember that it was odd or unusual. I was doing this for years. This was our normal.

The psychologist wrote throughout the report that his attention was variable, but she commented that verbal subtests tapping receptive language processing appeared more challenging for him, as he was quick to become distracted and much more active when asked to listen and then respond appropriately. What clearly stood out, though, was how she noted that when being given a two-step command, he lost the ability to perform the first step. For example, "Before you give me the truck, give me the car." Brenden responded by only giving her the car. He scored in the seventh percentile on verbal comprehension. However, on expressive subtests or naming vocabulary, he scored at the ninety-eighth percentile. He was focused on the task and was very attentive. He was able to provide labels for common items. Furthermore, when his nonverbal reasoning abilities were tested, he performed solidly in the average range. That would be in the area of a task that required him to assemble foam squares into the same shape as the clinician. One more time, she writes, however, that his distractibility rather than his receptive language difficulties compromised his availability to participate. Wait, what! This is inconceivable to me. I just don't understand. Where is she going with this? He is scoring in the seventh percentile for receptive language processing. He cannot follow a two-step direction. But his attention span is her focus. I didn't get this at the time. I didn't think being inattentive was anywhere on my top ten, because communication was my number one concern. If someone doesn't understand what is verbally being asked of them in a classroom or anywhere else for that matter, wouldn't that cause inattention to occur? Yet she concludes that because of her frequent prompting to listen carefully, his performance significantly improved. This, she stated, suggests that attention and sustained concentration likely plays a role in his processing of verbal information.

The YCAT (the Young Children's Achievement Test) was also administered to look at his current academic skills. Her findings were that his greatest weakness was in the area of spoken language. In the subtest, his score was sixty-nine. She expected his score to be in the average range of 103. She felt his other scores in other academic subtests were solid. His extremely low score in spoken language was reflective of his inattentive participation. The statement she uses to clarify this is: he was unable to look at a picture and point to the dog closest to the chair. He was unable to repeat verbatim a five-word sentence and three words read sequentially. So I am thinking that yes! Someone gets this: this is what I have been saying about him. Surely, there will be a light here at the end of this exhaustive assessment.

When the report arrived, the diagnostic impressions left me speechless: *314.00 attention deficit/hyperactivity disorder, predominantly inattentive type.* I remember asking her, how could this be? In light of his language delays, did she not think this was PDD (Pervasive Development Disorder)? I was so convinced based on his social and communicative problems. She stated that she absolutely thought that due to his symptoms of difficulty focusing and sustaining attention at school, he should be given a trial of a psychostimulant. She did allude to the fact that the language issues could be addressed educationally once the behavior was resolved. I just didn't agree. I went on to say that in fact he was Asian, and how many Asian kids had ADHD? She told me that it was rare, but she did see it at least once a year. She also suggested that we work with a behavioral therapist at AI Dupont, and participate in a parenting group, along with social groups for Brenden. Okay, well, I went for help. Now learn to accept the help, but my intuition said otherwise.

So with the newly printed report, I reluctantly shared it with the educational team at the school. I started my five-year-old on Adderall, an amphetamine because he had ADHD. Indeed, I am a good mother, and I need to give my little boy a stimulant so he can manage himself in the classroom. The more I read about this drug, the more I was skeptical. But I have to tell you, the trial was remarkable! I couldn't believe what I was seeing in and out of the classroom. He could actually sit at story time along with everyone else, without getting up and stomping on people and their papers. What kind of drug is this? Is this the answer? I went to see myself, and he seemed to be just what everyone wanted to see. He was just like the other kids. In fact, there was an activity where all he did was look at himself in the mirror and talk. He would use his hands to motion and make gestures. I remember the teacher enjoying that so much, like she had never before met Brenden. But I knew him by heart. There was no empathy, no understanding here. He was behaving like someone had turned his dial down to low. He was like a 16 2/3 RPM vinyl record spinning on a turntable. Where was his enthusiasm his purpose, his fortitude? It had been three weeks, and there was another meeting to discuss Brenden's progress.

April 2002, here we are to discuss the medication trial. The comments were as follows. "Brenden does not seem as frustrated or excitable in class now." "He is listening better." "At times, he is choosing to move to a table by himself so he can complete activities better." "He is more on track and accepting of himself now." Although I did agree, what was wrong with how this felt? When taken off the medications, how would he be in class? Peace, there was peace. He should at least deserve that, and since I was there daily, I could see he was most certainly more attentive and in a lower frustrated level. Here was the problem. I am in the classroom accommodating Brenden daily. At times, he needs one to one support, along with one-to-one instruction, with one-step directions. There needed to be a complete review of his educational needs. It was nearing the end of the year. My battle to keep speech and language services for summer or ESY (Extended School Year) was in play. To be honest, his weakness were so great in the area of spoken language I knew this was the immediate issue that had to be resolved. It was his difficulty with auditory directions and then being unable to express himself. I had to make this right. Something huge was missing. It was as if now, like Brenden, I was lethargic to solving the one-thousand-piece puzzle.

CHAPTER 5

PHONE A FRIEND

So I am not even sure how much time passed, but I am sure it did, and it sure did fly. I was consumed with finding the clarification to unlock the truth. I knew things were not quite right. ADHD? Brenden? What about his communication issues, his social issues? He was clearly struggling in class with turn taking and basically making friends. I talked to anyone and everyone about what to do. I read everything online about IEPs and goals and how to get that appropriate education. I read mostly at night after a very long day, and I was learning a little at a time about how to help my son. I was back to work now on a part-time basis and would often talk to my coworkers about what was going on with Brenden. A good friend asked me if I had ever heard about Dan Gottlieb from a radio show called *Voices in the Family*. She continued to tell me about him and his grandson, Sam, who had autism. Here is where I will tell you that people come into your life for a reason, and this I will believe in forever, fate is a friend of mine.

Dan Gottlieb is a psychologist, who was the host of a show called *Voices in the Family*.

He also is an author of a book that was an international bestseller, *Letters to Sam*. You see, his grandson Sam has autism, and when I read about Sam, he sounded a lot like Brenden. For example, in the book, it says, "There were tantrums that reached a level of uncontrolled violence when, for no obvious reason, he would repeatedly bang his forehead against the wall or floor." It also said, "Sam didn't speak until he was nearly four years old." So I think, *What would be the harm to actually e-mail Dan Gottlieb?* I really had nothing to lose, and in that moment, I felt that somehow I was connected to what they were living. The school was saying learning disability, but there was more to that. There was this new term called *autism*, and from what I was reading, Brenden had many of the signs. But he was six now. He was struggling more than ever now. He needed help *now*!

So I was very surprised when Dan Gottlieb actually responded to my e-mail. He even suggested that I talk with his daughter Debbie about my thinking so she could be a support for me. I cannot tell you how this transported me into another time and place where there was hope and there was kindness. Debbie called me, or I called her not sure about the details; but we were in touch, and she was validating everything in my mind. I was afraid, but I knew I was on the right track. I couldn't help but think Brenden was obsessed with the trains, and I was the conductor and had to get him on the right track. I needed a diagnosis; however, my own doctors didn't notice the signs. They suggested I get my doctors on board and then call around to see where I could have Brenden evaluated and screened for autism. Well, I did just that, but guess what, most facilities like Johns Hopkins and children's hospitals were only seeing cases up to the age of three. Brenden was six now. We were told we would have to wait a year. I decided, no, this could not devour us. I called on Dan Gottlieb yet again. He was the single best thing to come into our lives, and he got us the appointment that would set Brenden's future into motion. Dan Gottlieb and his daughter were the luminary individuals, who saw our family striving for accuracy and the gospel truth of what ailed our son. On January 6, 2003, we were at the place, the destination of a journey at the Children's Seashore House. Brenden was now six years and two months old. Other children were being seen and evaluated for autism up until the age of three. I was not afraid to go. I was not afraid to possibly hear the words *autism*. I felt it already. Enough time had been wasted. It would change everything, and I cried in anticipation of finally reaching him. That is when appropriate really had meaning for me. This was very appropriate and necessary. I have a picture of Brenden when he was six, and beside it is a plaque that said, "*Believe* . . ." and I did.

CHAPTER 6

OCCUPATIONAL THERAPY AND AUDITORY INTEGRATION TRAINING

As we waited for the results of the evaluation at the Seashore House, I invariably noticed daily that Brenden's sensory world was in total dysfunction. When he was in first grade and we awaited the results of the testing from the Seashore House, there was an occupational therapist assessing him at school. His motor coordination, self-care skills, and language comprehension were atypical, to say the least. If you compared him to a typical peer, which I did very often, the differences were alarming. When his fine motor skills were assessed, meaning his eye-hand coordination and dexterity, he scored only for a child who was four years old. The struggle here was that he was six years old. When asked to place pennies as quickly as possible on a square drawn on a piece of paper, he lost credit for the task due to his insistence to line them up perfectly, not quickly. His cutting was choppy, and coloring was age appropriate. He hated to color, and that never worried me at all, so if he colored outside the lines, I was contented that he just followed the directions and used the correct colors.

Incredibly, this therapist included a sensory motor functioning questionnaire from our home environment. Brenden showed areas of difference and severe problems with hypersensitivity to everyday stimuli. The greatest was his oral stimuli or indifference to foods and their textures. Commonly, any auditory input or certain sounds would also be a trigger, for example the fire alarm. Immediately, this therapist addressed these problems by teaching me to perform DPP or Deep Pressure Protocol. I was taught the Wilbarger Protocol and used a small soft surgical brush to his arms, legs, hands, and back to reduce his sensory defensiveness. It was a deep-pressure brush so to speak, more like a massage. Never would you brush the stomach or face. Afterward, I would have to do joint compressions to complete the procedure. Brenden loved it. The total time to do this was about three minutes. It had a great effect on him, so much so that I started to notice improvement in his motor coordination. I had bought an exercise ball, and he could never sit on it without falling, but after brushing, he was in so much more control. One night, he sat at the dinner table on the ball and was so balanced and comfortable, not defensive or awkward in his own skin! Brenden knew when to ask for a brush, and since he didn't receive this in school, I would have to do this at home, his days were long.

She also observed his gross motor coordination. She noted his difficulty with running, jumping, and skipping. He also walked down the stairs with a two-foot pattern, meaning he would place on foot, then the other on each step going up or down. She documented his low muscle tone and how he became anxious trying to learn new movement. Her connection was that his gross motor dysfunction was delayed and did affect his ability in physical education and in socializing with peers. Subsequently, his eye coordination and fine motor control would also be an issue, and then she recommended a physical therapy consult. This adventure of working with this talented therapist had left a lasting impression with us. Her contribution was key to moving in the manner of becoming unbroken, notably another miracle around us.

In her evaluation, this therapist went on to educate the staff about his hypersensitivities at school. She related his behavior to signal the staff that something was chaotic or noisy and his sensory system being unable to handle the stimuli and may cause him pain. Yes, pain in everyday experiences and removing him from them would minimize the offensive input. She also noted that it would be critical for the staff to understand this is not bad behavior but his way of trying to control his responses. This woman's passion for her work was another miracle around me. Everything I said or noticed, she validated and found a solution. She taught me how to help Brenden, and in a way, she stood up for me to the school. I would say these things all the time, but it would just be behavior to the staff. I felt exonerated for the first time and paramount to that Brenden was improving with her assistance.

Mysteriously enough, she also made note of his vision, where she found that he had difficulty with tracking and saccades. Tracking is how your eyes work together for reading words on a page from left to right or important for eye-hand coordination. The saccades is how your eyes move quickly and swiftly from one place to another, so again for reading words on a page. She found that he had difficulty controlling his eye movements. She encouraged me to look into a behavioral optometrist or someone who was certified in binocular vision. She explained that she was only licensed to do a screening. I had never heard of such a thing, but I trusted her, and since it was not a school-based service, Brenden would need yet another medical evaluation. This would turn into a critical fitting piece of this puzzle that I was shuffling around. Complex pieces for sure, with the degree of difficulty like an eighteen-thousand-piece puzzle.

Auditory Integration

Without a doubt, AIT changed things for the better. It was the best medicine in the world to a child who couldn't process infor-mation. I truly believed auditory processing was vital to Brenden's severe language disorder. Brenden always had a very low tolerance to certain sounds. Not all sounds, like music for example, was tolerable, even pleasant, to him. But other sounds like feet pounding on the gym floor were intolerable. I recall the very first day he had gym and came home screaming at me, "It hurts me!" "I am going to explode. Call someone. I can't do it!" I called his teacher to ask her what was happening in the class. She replied she was unaware of any problems. This pattern of manufactured responses like this would continue to harm Brenden all year long. His sensory processing was the trouble here. Just like his adverse reaction to being touched in gym class was occurring, the noise was an issue as well.

My cousin Flossie mailed me an article about a speech pathologist named Terrie Silverman. The article was named "Hearing Too Much." In the article, I learned about AIT. It was started by a French doctor (Berard) in the 1960s and brought to America. Annabel Stehli had mentioned how it helped her daughter in her book *The Sound of a Miracle*. It had been used by many families in New Jersey, especially ones with autism, who tend to block out all sensory information. The training itself was two half-hour sessions where the child would listen to music via headphones on a broad range of frequencies. The total time of treatment was ten days at a cost of about $1300.00. The music is tailored to individual songs from classical to rock. The child is basically listening to different sounds mixed together. This helps them filter the sounds and modulate them. Basically, you are conditioning the ears to process sound. I was astonished to also read that it could also develop parts of the brain that process language. I was interested, and I contacted Terrie. She told me there was no way to know if there would be success. However, it could improve balance, sleeping, and concentration. The first step would have to be an audiology appointment to determine the child's ability to tolerate the sound exposure.

I then got to talk to a family friend of my brothers, whose son did have the treatment. They did feel it had helped their son. However, they also said that even the slightest noise could erase all the good it does. In their case, it was a dish falling to the floor, and then it was back to square one. How alluring this was to me. I just felt we had to try. He was so tortured in that gym class. I had even gone out to get my own OT evaluation, which recommended an adaptive PE program. Nothing was done. I had to send him into that class every Monday. I would promise him I was working on a solution. He would plead not to go! One day, I said I would go to gym with him to help. When I got there, he said to me, "Don't come in, Mom." He didn't want his friends to see his mom with him in gym or trying to get him out of the class. I then watched as he joined his twenty-eight classmates and ran around the gym with pain over his face, holding his ears! So we had to find the money for the AIT treatment. It was our only chance, our only hope.

I read a lot about how the vestibular and auditory systems were related. In fact, in terms that everyone can understand, both their receptors are located in what is called your inner ear. The vestibular system is mostly about your head in space. Its purpose is to be aware of positions and motions of your head. So the connection here is movement and sound. Lots of kids with vestibular dysfunction also have auditory language issues. This was exactly one of Brenden's issues. Here are some signs to look for, taken from *The Vestibular System and Auditory Language Processing* by Carol Stock Kranowitz, MA.

- May seem unaware of the source of sound, and may look all around to locate where the sounds come from.
- May have trouble identifying voices or discriminating between sounds, like "bear" and "bore."
- May be unable to pay attention to one voice or sound without being distracted by other sounds.
- May be distressed by noises that are too loud, sudden, metallic, or high pitched, or sounds that don't bother others.
- May have trouble putting thoughts into spoken or written words.

These were the main problems I saw in Brenden, so AIT was risky but in my mind essential. So we went during the summer and met Terrie in West Chester for our two sessions a day. I remember the second session being much harder on him. I would ask, "Hey, what songs are you listening to back there?" He would always say, "I don't know." It was funny one day Terrie told me he was listening to Bob Dylan sing, "Everybody must get stoned,." and Brenden called out to her, "I have to lie down!" But he really did need to be careful. Initially, his balance was way off. He walked funny and said he felt dizzy, and of course, we were retraining that inner ear. Soon he was fine and tolerating the treatments.

Afterward, the change was remarkable. He was speaking clearly and processing what was said to him so much better. One night, I asked him what he wanted for dinner, and he replied, "What's available?" Astonishingly, Brenden began eating tangerines and cinnamon, and yes, he started dancing! Honestly, when people say there are miracles around you, there are. I felt this was one chance of a lifetime, all because my cousin sent me that article. So, yes, miracles are around you everywhere, even in your family members. Open your eyes to them, and you will acquire gratitude!

Brenden's Landscape: AIT

I can remember Terri. She had olive skin with wavy black hair. I would listen to music twice a day, in the morning and in the afternoon. I recall that I did this during the summer. It was 2004. It was the first time I was in West Chester. Was being in Chester County a sign that I would move there to further my education? An education that can be tinkered to my needs?

CHAPTER 7

THE OUTSIDE SPEECH EVALUATION

In September 2002, I took Brenden for an outside speech and language evaluation. I just felt even though he was receiving services at school three days a week, two individual and one group, it was not enough. I always knew that if he could just communicate better, he would be better. He was so frustrated and had just finished an eight-week behavioral course at AI Dupont. I attended the course myself, although the adults were not with the kids we were separated.

In fact, one of the coordinators of the program came to me to discuss Brenden's lack of expressive language. She maintained that he was having difficulty participating in the program and appeared frustrated at times with oral directions and social situations. She wanted to know if he was enrolled in a speech and language program, and I told her he was receiving that in school. I recall just standing there waiting for her to say something profound like, "Hey, your kid doesn't have ADHD. Isn't anyone concerned with his language delay?" As I stood there, I thought, yes, if a perfect stranger to me can see it, then I will pursue this road less traveled. I will look into that and go outside the school and see what other professionals had to say.

So down to AI Dupont we went, yet again. This time, I had my daughter, Emily, with me.

Did I forget to talk about her? I didn't mean to. She is one of the reasons I saw things that were delayed in Brenden. Emily taught me how to love, her kindness, warmness, and pure genuineness. No one I knew possessed her refreshing spirit. She revived my strength, and that made everyone's life fulfilled. She would be my strength, but she would also relinquish so much, more than she was asked perhaps.

AUTISM IS LIKE LOOKING THROUGH A WINDOW

My brother Brenden has this thing called Autism. Autism affects your brain, and it is called a disability. Autism affects your eyes, sometimes it makes you have to get glasses, well only for small words. My brother has a pair of glasses. Sometimes we fight but we get over it. Some days we play together with our neighbor Maddy. Usually we play sports, hockey, football and baseball. Maddy and I are called the Ice creamers' hockey team, and we play with Brenden. They are all fun and my favorite one to play with Brenden is badminton. Even though sometimes it is hard to talk to Brenden when we are playing, I still love him very much!

I think he has the coolest room. He has blue walls, and a bulletin board over his bed. He has about nine or ten sports pennants that he hangs there. He is the best because he helps my mom. He lifts things that are heavy, like the wash and furniture. He also likes to laugh all the time. I really do not want him to get lost, so I make sure I know where he is. I always worry about him, and he is my favorite person to play with. Brenden has a flag collection of state flags, and he likes to wave them a lot. He likes to listen to music in the car, and his favorite songs are from the1980's.

Brenden needs social skills. When my friends are over, I show him good social skills. Sometimes I give him ideas for words to say. I look out for him, and I care about him so much. I guess you could say that I love him! I want to help other kids with Autism. Last year when I was in first grade, my mom and I read My Friend With Autism to our class. We made puzzle pieces for what we learned that day. I try to help others understand why loud noises hurt Brenden's ears, and why he needs to wear headphones. I try to help him with his school projects, so he doesn't get frustrated.

I like Brenden the way he is, and I don't want him to change. When you meet someone who may be different from the others, you shouldn't ask if they have Autism. You should wait and learn what they like a lot, then you can see who they are inside.

I think Autism is like looking through a window, because you can stop and see what there is to look at, and this is how they learn. I think by helping them look in the window we can all make a difference. This is how I know I am making a difference, every day.

Emily wrote that when she was in second grade, she was a finalist in literature that year, but she is always a winner in my book!

Brenden was age five and ten months now, the evaluation showed that his expressive language functioning was at age three years and eleven months. Although his receptive skills were within normal limits, they did pick up on difficulties . . . following directions, sentence imitation, and understanding passive voice quality. They recommended therapy for forty-five minutes for two to three individual sessions. His goals included learning to follow two-step directions and answering *wh* questions. One thing they did say and instruct me to do was to have home practice, and I thought *yes*! Someone guiding me to habitually institute a wraparound plan to build his communication deficits. She told me to have activities that helped him practice his two-to-three-step directions. Repeating it if necessary with visuals, then having Brenden repeat the steps to me. Ask him *why* and *when* questions throughout the day, describe what you are doing in complete sentences so he can improve his sentence length. In her words, she stated, "Goals need to include expressive, receptive language as well as articulation." "Language is much more a concern at this time." They also noted that if parental concerns should continue regarding a diagnosis, an appointment with a developmental pediatrician would be recommended. Miraculously, there it was again. Look further, look deeper, so that is exactly what I did.

CHAPTER 8

DEVELOPMENTAL PEDIATRIC EVALUATION

According to the Autism Society, "ASD or autism spectrum disorder is a complex developmental disability; signs typically appear during early childhood and affect a person's ability to communicate, and interact with others . . . Some of the behaviors associated with autism include delayed learning of language; difficulty making eye contact or holding conversation; difficulty with executive functioning, which relates to reasoning and planning; narrow, intense interests; poor motor skills' and sensory sensitivities . . . The diagnosis of autism spectrum disorder is applied based on analysis of all behaviors and their severity."

Okay, so there it is in writing, and for the last six years and two months, I knew it in my heart. The evaluation itself was something I was a part of, not in a participatory way, but I could sit with Brenden and watch. The doctor conducted the Autism Diagnostic Observation Schedule module 2. Brenden did not have the language capabilities to be fluent, so he was administered this module. It was sessions of some structured tasks, which always involved some type of a social action being observed between the person conducting the exam and Brenden. They also scrutinized his communicative performance. Most of the testing was done at a child's table where the examiner would ask him to play with a certain toy or make-believe play. That didn't go well. I remember him just sitting there looking at the toys, not even looking at the person making the requests. Whenever there was a conversation, he seemed to lack the ability to respond or react. And to be honest, I do not think he looked at the examiner at all. When they offered him a snack, he didn't even eat it, not a preferred food. I think it was a Graham cracker. You could say he didn't interact at all. He would look to me at times, but he never said a word, maybe just *mom*. I smiled at him and reassured him everything was fine, but inside, I was not fine. It was hard to watch him, and even though he was very tuned in so to speak, he was struggling. I told the doctor how he reads the encyclopedia, merely to get information. His long-term memory was exceptional; however, he was indifferent to his peers at school and had severe problems with pragmatic conversation. I told her that he had compulsions like having his shirt being tucked in, always. He always had a hat on and wore the same boots, along with his spellbinding interest in making items out of paper. I remember saying that Brenden always had to use the bathroom at the same time every day. I said, "Is that normal, to have to go to the bathroom at the same time every day?" The doctor just looked at me. I guess she was thinking it was fine or normal or didn't have an opinion on the topic. But when you see this on a daily basis, you have to wonder about the control factor there. It was those routines that I was referring to. This also coincided with meals, smelling everything, always the same foods, never trying anything new. Unable to adapt to changes and the universal hand flapping, flag waving that he participated in. In looking back, it really made him happy to wave flags. He would love a good windy day and just hold that flag high, long may it wave. I suppose he was thinking. It was soothing, peaceful to him. It must have quieted his world. So in retrospect not a bad thing, but perhaps a sign of the trouble he felt within, that he would have to retreat like that.

I completed the Australian Scale for Asperger Syndrome, which was significant for many symptoms that were atypical. For example, on a scale of 1-6, I rated his lack of understanding of how to play with other children at a 6. That he was indifferent to peer pressure, did not follow what other children are doing, used less eye contact, and was fascinated by particular objects.

Upon physical exam, the doctor noted that Brenden's head was two standard deviations above the normal. She never really explained what that had to do with anything, and honestly, she was the only doctor to say anything about it. I just figured that in the scheme of things, the size of his head was not that big of an issue. However, I had no knowledge that a head circumference below or above the normal was almost always associated with a neurological disorder. So having microcephaly can contribute to lack of brain development. Since Brenden was adopted, I really had no idea of his family history or if even in fact the medical records were accurate. So fragmented, yet here we were, and the next appointment would be the feedback session. That would be the turning point of his future.

I drove to the feedback session alone. I remember everyone asking me if I wanted company. I did not. I was fine to go alone. I already felt the diagnosis coming and felt this would just be a formality. The doctor stated,

> *Although formally Brenden has symptoms in the autism spectrum, he should probably be seen as a child who has a primary language disorder, whose autistic-like or Asperger symptoms appear largely to be a result of compensation for his very severe difficulties with understanding and responding to language.*
>
> *Since language also mediates socialization and most social interactions as well as learning, pragmatic language skills and social skills training should be the primary targets of his interventions.*
>
> *With the diagnosis of autistic spectrum disorder, be it Asperger's or PDD, Brenden becomes eligible for additional therapeutic interventions, focusing on socialization and pragmatics skills. I am, therefore, referring him for wraparound services coordination of intensive behavioral, sensory pragmatic language, occupational and physical therapy, and am referring his parents for support.*

So there it was *autism*. I cried on the way home but not because of sadness; I was elated. I was relieved. I was going to get things right for him. I knew that the first evaluation, although helpful, just didn't capture everything that was going on neurologically. I was so grateful for everyone who gave me information, a tip, a lead, or even just hearing these words, "Did you know?" That is how I got to this day, and now it was time to fine-tune things. There was no more time to waste, and I decided that we would take the road less traveled.

CHAPTER 9

PRIMARY LANGUAGE DISORDER

I decided that that one particular line in the report was going to be my guiding light, and I did truly feel that is was the most important thing to focus on. So I realized that only having speech in school couldn't possibly be enough if you have to learn to communicate and you have autism. So I looked at our insurance a little more carefully to see what could and what would be covered, and it turned out to be the best thing I ever did. *We* met Emily, the speech pathologist who recommended a thirty-minute session, once a week. Now at first, I was, like, is that enough? You bet it was, because the beauty of this was the fact that I could watch; this was brilliant! It was something like a blanket of hope all wrapped up into a thirty-minute session. I wasn't in the room with him. They had a private room where you could watch through a one-way mirror. And in that short time frame, I could see the progress and how Brenden would respond and improve his ability to communicate. The therapist worked on goals to answer *wh* questions, like *who, what, where, why,* and *when.* She increased his eye contact not based on telling him to look at her; she gave him verbal cues or played a game where she incorporated making eye contact. Brenden would talk to her using nouns and plurals, subjects, and verbs. All I could think of was when his school goal was to have one word in a sentence, and now he was speaking them. Brenden truly loved Emily. She was kind and soft-spoken, and it didn't seem like work to him, because it was enjoyable. Brenden willingly went to every appointment, and this was after school when he was tired. My favorite goal of hers was the one where he would sequence events and tell about daily events and stories. She helped him sequence five to six events, and there it was; he was telling a story, and I got to see that!

After six months, Brenden increased his comprehension and answered *wh* questions with 66 percent accuracy, mastered stating the function of a noun by 90 percent, and used plurals 80 percent of the time. In a sentence, he used the correct subject-verb agreement 75 percent of the time but needed visual cues, and the best of all, he made substantial improvement using visual maps to tell a story. For six months, Brenden went for that thirty minutes, but then our insurance would not cover any further treatment. But I would never regret that, because it was a rainbow of hope; it was progress in a sea of uncertainty. This paper I saved explains clearly how the struggle was real.

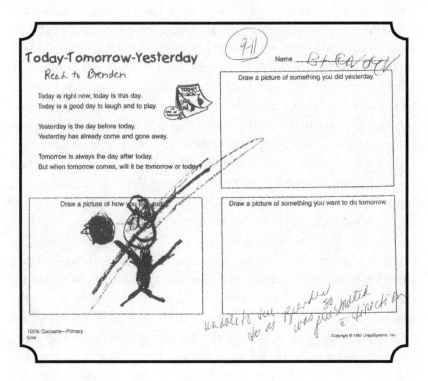

In this worksheet, titled "Today, Tomorrow and Yesterday," Brenden was so frustrated. He could not understand this sheet as it was read to him. Even as I read it, I could understand how difficult the concept of time was so perplexing.

Today is right now; today is this day.
Today is a good day to laugh and play.
Yesterday is the day before today.
Yesterday has already come and gone away.
Tomorrow is always the day after today.
But when tomorrow comes, will it be tomorrow or
today?

As you can see, he attempted to draw a picture of how he looked today. Sadly, he had either no idea of what he did yesterday, including what he planned on doing tomorrow. Read that aloud to yourself. I didn't even know who was on first. The trouble here was he still had significant weaknesses in receptive and expressive language. The school speech therapist's notes at the annual review stated temporal concepts were difficult including who what where when questions, with why questions cues were needed. Expressively, he was able to make a sentence with only five to six words in length, he had limited spontaneous verbalization, and to compare and contrast things, he needed cues as well. But with summer break approaching, there would still be work to be done. The therapist also did say that Brenden wanted to make conversation and that he could rhyme words now. At this time, we discussed the need for extended year services. As I described in detail how Brenden regressed with language skills during periods of sickness or time off from school and that it was a critical life skill for him. I was told that no one else noticed that he became frustrated when he couldn't communicate what he needed. The speech therapist then stated her data indicated he was progressing with his language skills. She said that he was at risk in the following areas:

- Following two- and three-step commands

- Describing remote events
- Producing complete sentences
- Answering *wh* questions, especially *why* questions

I remember sitting there thinking, *He's not frustrated?* I insisted that he was and should be eligible for extended school year services based on all of the risks to speech and language. I pondered why they would question a critical skill of producing a complete sentence, something that could be put on hold over summer break? Somehow, I was able to advocate for extended year services. There would be a meeting later in the year to develop an IEP, which there was. However, when I received the paperwork stating the speech services, there was a sticky note that read, "I forgot to put the six weeks on the service page of the IEP. "A maximum of six weeks is what we are allowed to recommend for students needing ESY services." That seemed a little fractured to me. Technically, Brenden would only have half of the summer in speech sessions. I felt that they were limiting the duration and therefore the amount of services by saying six weeks. Even at the meeting, it seemed vague; however, I assumed it would continue as delivered in the school year. So this became my first stab at writing a formal complaint to the state. I always had the procedural guidelines, but now it was up to me to implement them. Initially, I had to absolutely look up the IDEA (Individuals with Disabilities Education Act) and its regulations. This is so accessible and simple to acquire, and it's free. You can download it or ask for a free copy from the Department of Education. I highly recommend this to be placed on your reading list. What I decided was that I wanted to file a complaint based on Part B of the IDEA. This covered my child as he was receiving special education services and was age three to twenty-one. My child was entitled to FAPE (Fair and Appropriate Education), and this issue, in my opinion, was violating his rights to that education. What I educated myself about was that under the IDEA, there could not be a limit on duration, because it violates meeting the needs of the child. There are many reasons for the delivery of ESY. Often, there is regression and the inability to recoup skills once school returns in session. There is also emerging skills that could be documented and therefore needing current services to see them to fruition.

The issues subject to my investigation yielded the following facts:

- I alleged that the school limited the duration of ESY services.
- The school responded that the person who explained ESY services to me did so incorrectly.
- The determination was also made that with the exception of one student who received ESY for eight weeks. All other children received services for six weeks only.
- The discussion and conclusions were the following:
- If the IEP team determines that ESY services are required for the provision of FAPE, the public agency must ensure those services are available. In implementing this requirement, the public agency may not unilaterally limit the type, amount, or duration of ESY services.
- Because the evidence also showed that with the exception of one student, seventy-eight students also only received ESY for a total of six weeks as well, it suggested the school personnel did not have a clear understanding of the requirement.
- Therefore, based upon review of the data, the state determined the school had a practice of limiting the duration of time for students received ESY services.

This is the corrective action:

The school knowing the results of the investigation had reached out to me to remedy the situation. It was agreed that Brenden would receive four additional sessions of speech therapy, and upon completion, the team would meet to discuss progress. This was my first victory. I can only tell you that the feeling of winning something this great was also supported in receiving the progress gained. From March of 2003 to September 2003, the breakthrough for Brenden was staggering.

- *Wh* questions were now answered at 100 percent accuracy.
- From limited spontaneous recall to describing remote events with 40 percent completed thoughts
- Following two-step directions with 80 percent accuracy, and three step at 80 percent
- Using complete thoughts when started with word cues at 40 percent
- Using -*ed* past endings in sentences, 90 percent

I was learning what an appropriate education should look like, but I also was learning as I worried, stressed, and fought my way around a system of paperwork. The significance of the lessons learned was priceless. I would make many mistakes, but I would never ever give up, as Brenden was entering third grade. After that very first day of school, he told me about his day for the very first time. He was communicating in sentences now, a miracle. The adventure had just begun.

CHAPTER 10

The Good Stuff

Through the early school years, there were moments or comments that I wrote down, and I am so glad I did. I highly recommend this because the focus was always most often on the weaknesses of Brenden. It wasn't intentional, but the progress reports and teacher comments were undeniably not consistent with strengths, and of course, I understood that in order to show progress, you needed to know what to work on. But it is hard as a parent to endure, so when I would see or he would tell me something profound, I did take the time to jot that down, and when you pause to look at that, hope emerges.

While in his first elementary school, Brenden talked about Mrs. Peacock, who was his special education teacher. Brenden told me she "understood autism. I like it when we are together . . .When I leave here, I will miss her." He also spoke of Mrs. Hamilton, who taught Brenden quite a lot about sign language. In fact, in times of great frustration with language, he would be able to sign, and that saved him on many an occasion. We still have a book that we created with sign language. It was key to sustaining him. As Brenden put it, "I couldn't find the words." Even if it was only a word or a phrase, signing allowed him the capability to communicate. He needed that, and she gave him that tool. We were so grateful. I remember telling the principal how it had changed his world.

In the winter of 2003, I nominated Brenden for the Temple Grandin Award through Future Horizons. I felt as if he needed to have recognition for all of his hard work. He could relate to Temple, especially watching her Sensory Challenges video. He won that award and received a plaque and money for his education. As they wrote in the letter, rising above the challenges was commendable, and that due to the successes in his life, he was an inspiration to others.

He also was involved in a project of a student at John Hopkins, who received a grant to raise community awareness about autism. She created the Autism Netverse, where she showcased poetry, sketches, paintings, and photographs. Brenden submitted some sketches he did on Cal Ripken from the Orioles, his favorite team. He titled it "Play like Cal." This was such an exciting time for him. He loved to draw, and this really helped his self-worth. I was grateful to Vandna Jerath for the opportunity, and so was Brenden. He also got to go to an Orioles game, and Jeff Conine presented Brenden with his signed Jersey. Brenden got to go down on the field to receive it. He was elated and still has the Jersey today.

Brenden also was able to say profound things, like this for example: one day, he was referring to a behavior program in the school called Kelso's choices. Kelso was a frog, and there was a wheel of choices to empower kids to decide whether it was a big problem or a little problem. Brenden was talking about his friend John, who used Kelso's choices, and how proud he was of him. He also verbalized that he did not particularly like Kelso for autistic kids, because Kelso was a frog. He said frogs don't need to make any choices or decide about their problems. It made no sense to him. He also called kids like him (SP) special people; he called regular kids (NP) normal people. He always said he didn't belong with the NP kids, because he didn't understand what they were doing. He said they are not signing or using any pictures.

During this time, I connected with the CDC and their campaign Learn the Signs Act Early. I felt that both Brenden and I needed to give back. There were so many times that I sat in a doctor's office filled with frustration and confusion, knowing something was wrong with him. I felt this campaign helped doctors and parents work together to ensure each child would reach their full potential. We participated in health care professional distribution week. Brenden and I went in person to local doctors and handed out kits that contained pamphlets for patients and their families that said exactly what the signs were for autism. It also gave information about resources for help. Many doctors stated that they didn't know where to find this information and were very receptive to handing it out to parents and caregivers. Having Brenden with me made an impact as well. They could see how autism affected his life and yet were able to see that early detection and intervention meant success.

We were honored to be chosen for the partner spotlight. We were campaign champions! My favorite part of the article was my statement that when Brenden was frustrated with language, he would always say to me, "Help me find the words." That is what I always seem able to do for him, help him find the words, and I am not going to stop anytime soon.

This was an important cause for both of us, and I am proud that we could participate.

That's the good stuff for now. There is more good stuff later, of course after I start to open a can of worms.

CHAPTER 11

KIDSPIRATION

I started to wonder about Brenden's writing. Beyond the fine motor difficulties, he appeared to have great difficulty starting a sentence and planning and completing a summary based on what he just read. It was like his thoughts were not organized so that he could transfer them to paper. Strangely enough, he could verbalize things so much better now, but there was a disconnection when involving written work. Since he was in private speech sessions, he was introduced to a software program called Kidspirations. Emily, the therapist, used this program with Brenden, and I downloaded it as a free trial for use at home. He could use visuals to enhance and help with sentence structure. He could create vocabulary and a story web to sequence a story he read. I started to preread each story to him that he would be learning in class in second grade. We would then work on Kidspirations to prepare him for the week ahead. Not only did this help with learning, but it alleviated his anxiety. Here is some information from the website:

> Using visual thinking methodologies, Kidspiration provides a cross-curricular visual workspace for K-5 learners. Students combine pictures, text, numbers and spoken words to develop vocabulary, word recognition, reading for comprehension, writing and critical thinking

skills. With Kidspiration, students use graphic organizers to express thoughts and explore ideas and relationships. They create graphic organizers including webs, concept maps and Venn diagrams to clarify thoughts, organize information, apply new knowledge and build critical thinking skills.

3,000+ symbols in Kidspiration's Symbol Library provide visual support for concepts taught in K-5 language arts, social studies and science. Students can also import symbols from other sources. Symbol Search helps students search and find just the right symbols to express their thoughts and ideas.

In November 2003, I asked the school for an AT (assistive technology) evaluation, to determine if technology would help Brenden. They were using story starters, templates, and graphic organizers to help with his writing; but I wondered, why not technology? His teacher Barbara Glessner was marvelous with him, she really was, and very open to suggestions. Brenden did extremely well in her class, both academically and socially that year. Second grade was a gift! But the person doing the assessment felt that he was accessing the curriculum using low-tech AT accommodations just fine. She did note, however, that during an assessment Brenden was having trouble formulating a response to a question, and she suggested that the teacher scribe his response, instead of having him write it. The teacher reported that Brenden had done marginally better when he dictated his responses. But this was not registering with the evaluator. In fact, she felt that in some way it was the voice inflection and cues from the teacher that was helping Brenden. I felt that I had no choice to accept that for now, but I knew and, in fact, saw how Kidspirations helped him at his private speech lessons; and at home, I would continue to work with Brenden the best I could. This was going to be a long haul.

In February of the next year, I again requested that Brenden be evaluated to use the Kidspirations software. Although the report stated that data had been collected on a variety of writing assignments, only two assignments were given to him with the use of Kidspirations. When he wrote himself, they stated that he needed very few verbal prompts. However, the report neglects to mention the other supports the teacher gave him during the assignment such as helping to think, having him verbally voice his ideas, prompting to change things in his writing that didn't make sense, and writing very basic sentences. In order for Brenden to complete a writing assignment, he needed word cards, graphic organizers, sentence starters, and writing templates. Out of eight assignments, he only completed one independently. Only two assignments were attempted on Kidspirations, and because they took one and a half hours to complete and needed verbal prompts, she stated that he was not able to use this software independently. At an IEP meeting to review these results, they told me to expose him to this at home and give him the option of using it at home. Again, I felt as if I was alone in the quest to help him, especially with writing, which was so frustrating to him. At night especially, he would complain about his hands hurting and that his handwriting was not neat. There was no vision here. He could write faster than he could type, so he would not have the benefit of technology. It did not connect that his difficulty with sentence structure would make writing difficult. He may have known significant details but be unable to describe what he just saw, and unless cued, he could not sequence events. In addition, he would have an error in responding to *wh* questions without a clue or picture. This is why having pictures would help him, and Kidspirations did all of this. Here's an example of the work Brenden and I completed at home. I wasn't worried about the time it took to type. He would get better at that in time, but this was what he needed to work independently and have less frustration and anxiety. We would revisit technology in school when we found ourselves in that place where instructional methods were adapted to the learning styles of students on the spectrum. It would also have to be where a parent was supported and recognized as a valued partner in their child's education. Does that place exist? We would soon find out that it did exist, if you look hard enough!

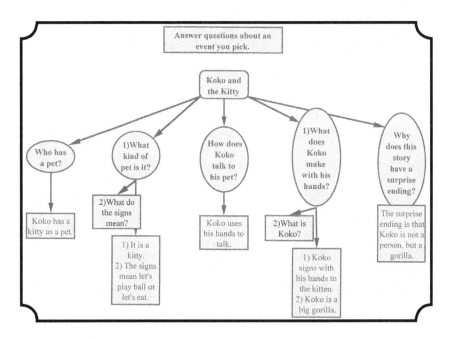

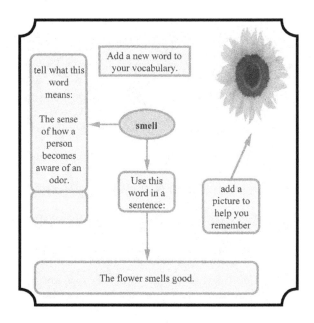

Brenden's Landscape

As a child in the early 2000s, using a computer was like going to the moon. I felt like I had been the chosen one. Now that I see this diagram today, I can also see how it helped me.

CHAPTER 12

Vision Therapy

It was December of 2005, and since June of that year, I had grave concerns about Brenden's reading, and somehow, his vision seemed off. I also started to see him have difficulty with his eye control. On regular visual exams, he was unable to discriminate between line 4 and 5. In math, I noticed that he was copying numbers over others when regrouping. All previous eye exams had shown nothing, but they were just normal vision examinations, and his last had been at AI Dupont after he failed his school eye test. I started to research the Internet for any information on vision changes related to autism. I found plenty of information, and the vision I am speaking of is binocular vision. This cannot be tested on a regular eye exam. This is the information I read on a website:

> A binocular vision impairment is any visual condition wherein binocular visual skills are inadequately developed. A comprehensive eye examination should include the testing of these important binocular visual skills:
>
> - Tracking: the ability to move the eyes across a sheet of paper
> - Fusion: the ability to use both eyes together at the same time

- Stereopsis: binocular depth perception
- Convergence: the ability of the eyes to move and work as a team
- Visual Motor Integration: the ability to transform images from a vertical to a horizontal

After seeing this, I immediately knew that was what Brenden was struggling with. So I searched doctors who were trained to perform this type of exam, and I found her. The binocular exam revealed that he had intermittent alternating exotropia with low base in and out vergence ranges. That meant that he had difficulty adjusting his eyes in a classroom from near to far, or for example from the paper on his desk to the chalkboard. He also had very low accommodative facility, which meant words were blurry and he could not focus. The biggest issue was that he had convergence insufficiency, which involves using your eyes as a team while doing near work or reading. As he read for an extended period of time, he was unable to fuse the images together, and the words were all blurry. Eye strain and headaches were the symptoms he was complaining of. It also meant that while reading, words would move on a page. This made comprehension extremely difficult. She recommended vision therapy to train his eyes to work together. It would strengthen his eye muscles and recoordinate his visual system.

I was elated! I knew there was a reason, but I felt so terrible that I had let this go on since June. I really liked the doctor, and the therapy session were initially really hard for Brenden. He did complain about one exercise where he had to put pegs into holes on a spinning wheel. Well, actually, he hated it, but as always he did it. He actually got better and had less visual complaints. He had to also be trained to take visual breaks as well while reading, to avoid eye fatigue. She explained it to him that it would be the same as carrying a heavy bag and needing to stop. He needed to stop his near work and look out far. This was hard for him to do while in school. We also had work to do at home, because he didn't go to therapy every day, only three days a week. So we would do eye exercises, in addition to what was done in therapy. The dire straits of it all was that the school had no idea what I was talking about, and that was a huge problem, and that problem was escalating.

In 2010, I was researching visual impairment on the Internet, and I came across a project under way in the UK called the Visual Impairment and Autism project. They recognized that kids on the spectrum with a wide variety of impairment visually also would have an increased difficulty learning as well. They actually were connecting that often these two disabilities did exist and in fact understood that in order to understand the spoken language they would also need to see it in print. Needing enlarged print, or even braille, would be not the easiest to do or to refer to quickly. We were interviewed and decided to be part of the study. Most of the kids were in educational settings some more severe than others. But we were happy to share our story of how and where we found support. This was pretty exciting for Brenden, and he was walking on air showing his vision support and other teachers the article.

Parent's voices: VI, autism, and the route to diagnosis

Three parents share their stories of how and where they found support for their child with VI and autism.

Britt Fox

Joshua was born at 39 weeks and weighed just less than 6lb. He didn't feed at all following his birth and as his blood sugar levels dropped, he was admitted into the Special Care Baby Unit. From there he made good progress and within a week he was out and we were allowed to take him home.

We had no idea that there was anything wrong with his sight until we went for a routine check up with his paediatrician who said that he'd like to refer us to an ophthalmologist to be on the safe side. The ophthalmologist said that there were no obvious problems, but that he would like to refer us to a paediatric ophthalmologist for a second opinion. So, two weeks later when Joshua was 14 weeks old, we went to Birmingham Children's Hospital where Joshua had to have a general anaesthetic so that they could complete a full and comprehensive range of tests. When the paediatric ophthalmologist came back up on to the ward, he explained that Joshua's vision was 'seriously compromised'. Once we had time to take the information on board, we discovered that Joshua had an eye condition called persistent hyperplastic primary vitreous which in essence means that he is totally blind.

We always had a sixth sense about Joshua having more difficulties than 'just' being blind. When we spoke to his pre-school about our concerns they assured us that a lot of the behaviours we were concerned about (hand flapping / tiptoe walking / grimacing / echolalia / echopraxia) were all features of a blind child.

When Joshua started at school, we voiced the same concerns and were given the same reply – each of the behaviours was typically seen in a blind child and not to worry.

As Joshua got older his range of behaviours grew. We'd implement lots of strategies to combat an inappropriate behaviour only to have Joshua replace it with another!

When he started at his specialist school (The West of England School) we were offered an appointment with the paediatrician who visited there. She agreed that there were too many behaviours to be a coincidence and when we completed the DISCO (Diagnostic Interview for Social and Communication Disorders) questionnaire, everyone was amazed that we had gone this long without a diagnosis! It was such a relief to know that we weren't overprotective parents making a fuss about nothing; he really did have more difficulties than everyone first thought.

Despite facing challenges every day, Joshua is now at happy, healthy 17 year old College student who loves music, food and people!

Kate Curry

Realizing Brenden was a child with autism and now a visual impairment was very frustrating for him. He had to work extremely hard throughout the day in all classes.

researched on the internet and found that certain optometrists could identify reading issues with a comprehensive binocular vision exam, and if warranted, do vision therapy. Brenden had convergence problems, tracking, focusing and eye teaming problems. Often he would have headaches at school, and now we knew why. He had vision therapy several times. However the eye strain every day was significant during the school year. He needs to wear bifocal glasses while reading. We requested that the school involve the Chester County Intermediate Unit and evaluate him for a visual impairment. He qualified for services and this has changed his life. At first, he used large print text and books on tape, this was successful but as he moved into middle school, having the materials at hand during class became an issue.

Brenden's vision teachers have moved Brenden into digital capabilities and he travels through the school using multiple programs in all classes. In the middle and now high school, Brenden uses a 17 inch (43.18 cm) laptop computer with several programs to choose from. The program he uses most often is Adobe Reader. He uses it for its accessibility to PDF's, scanned-in worksheets, and his digital textbooks. He will also use Kurzweil 3000 for Windows, this assistive technology reads the text to him, and he can magnify the percentage to decrease eye strain. There are also tools that he uses such as a highlighter. Another option is Zoom Text, and Brenden compares that to using different lenses of glasses. He also uses a hand held reading device, so he can read away from the computer in a more comfortable setting.

His favourite technology is Dragon Naturally Speaking 10. This voice recognition software assists him with verbal responses when writing and typing is too difficult as the computer screen does cause eye strain at times. All of these technologies have helped him overcome barriers to reading due to his visual impairment. He now is advanced in reading but also does very well in all other courses of study. Reading is now fun for him, it is no longer stressful or frustrating, he is no longer behind in reading, or in any class for that matter!

Cheryl Hughes

My son was diagnosed at six weeks of age with an under-developed optic nerve. His condition was not fully explained and 13 years ago we didn't have access to the internet like we do today and we struggled to research his condition and understand the implications. At two and a half years old he was placed in a special needs nursery/school but as he grew older the environment became too challenging. He was diagnosed with autism at age 10 and we started to investigate independent 'autistic specific' schools and took it through the tribunal process. As part of the process, our son was examined by a consultant ophthalmic surgeon who diagnosed him with a 'cortex visual impairment'. The ophthalmology department offered great support and from undertaking our own research via the internet and purchasing specialist literature, this gave us great insight into our son's condition and helped us to understand and relate to him. We were able to develop a SEN statement that detailed our son's needs, objectives and provision and we have been able to secure an appropriate education placement, which he has recently started and thoroughly enjoys. ■

CHAPTER 13

THE DETERIORATION

Since it was the 2004–2005 school year, it was time for a third-grade education, and, boy, was I about to get one. This year would turn out to be the worst for Brenden but for me the tipping point, the division you might say. It also was during the time that my husband was fighting for our country in Iraq. I was alone in this battle at home. I had my family supports and of course my friends, but this catastrophe was rearing its ugly head. I wrote a lot of letters to the school this year for several reasons. I was floundering in my correspondences. I was trying to get my points across and literally was flying by the seat of my pants. I guess I could say my letters were very factual and to the point but not taken seriously. At times, I suppose the letters were written with such emotion that they came off as obnoxious. Knowledge is a very powerful thing, and the more I read, the more I realized things were not exactly how they should and could be. I started to really look at the IEP, and what the present levels of performance represent. According to the IDEA, each child's IEP must contain

> A statement of the child's present levels of academic achievement and functional performance, including

(1) how the child's disability affects the child's involvement and progress in the general education curriculum (i.e., the same curriculum as for nondisabled children); or

(2) for preschool children, as appropriate, how the disability affects the child's participation in appropriate activities.

I didn't feel Brenden's present levels were being captured to reflect his ability, strength, performance, and what he needed. Was there enough objective data so that the appropriate goals, services, and supports could be written? The present levels really drive the educational plan, and Brenden's were not getting the job done. His anxiety was building, and the teacher was tumultuous. I guess you could say he feared her, and that just brought more anxiety. For kids on the spectrum, fitting into everyday occurrences that are quite simple to us can appear very complex to them. When you have limited higher-level thinking skills, there is a lot of confusion. Making inferences are hard; coupled with a language disorder, the barriers are huge. They are literal thinkers, and the use of idioms like "Don't judge a book by its cover" makes things almost impossible to understand but not unattainable.

In November of that year, I had an outside occupational therapy evaluation done because in my eyes his issues were mostly sensory. He also was having difficulty with social issues. His current plan did not address his struggle with social cues, empathy, and appropriate conversation. Brenden was also complaining that while in gym, it "hurt my ears real bad." A sensory profile was done and revealed that he was hypersensitive to many typical everyday forms of stimulation. He had a low threshold for many types of input, especially auditory, visual, touch, and oral. As a result, he would try to avoid any situation he acknowledged overwhelming for him. I agreed wholeheartedly. I had to cut the tags out of his clothes just so he could wear them. The therapist stated that for Brenden leaving the tags in his shirts all day would be like a typical person hearing nails on a chalkboard continuously throughout the day.

She also said that he was unable to separate noises he was hearing in the background—like computers humming, classes changing—from what the teachers were saying.

The school's response was not supportive. They conducted an OT evaluation of their own, and the recommendation was not that of a sensory diet for Brenden at school and support while in gym class. In fact according to every teacher, Brenden was functioning "typically" throughout the day, except when in physical education. When speaking with the gym teacher, she reported to the therapist that Brenden had weak muscles, tires easily, had a weak grasp, and poor endurance. The therapist stated that I was the only one that was reporting sensory differences and that I should discuss my concerns with my doctor.

I went to the school one day to see Brenden during gym. While he was running laps with his peers, the look on his face was one of pain. Did anyone look at his face? Is it typical to be looking like that as you run? The outside OT evaluation I submitted suggested an adaptive PE program. This was never discussed. Shortly after this, at an IEP meeting, the teacher reported that Brenden was not reading on grade level, when on his first marking period she had stated he was on grade level. Again, I felt there was a missing link to what was happening with him. I decided to have an educational evaluation of my own completed. The school lacked the initiative, and they didn't seem to recognize how to educate someone who was autistic. I had to keep searching for the resources. Brenden had so much stress to deal with. At night, I would just let him talk at the dinner table and then ask all the *wh* questions to get to the bottom of it. My daughter was in pre-K at the time, and all she would talk about was the water table, and how she did at her stations. It was so sweet to hear of her involvement and successes of her day, while Brenden could only say, "I didn't know what _____ wanted?" "I think he wants to get me in trouble." Apparently, a boy in his class was making faces at him. Was he trying to be funny? Perhaps, but again his ability to read social cues was poor at best. When I brought this to the teacher's attention so that it could be resolved, all I was told was Brenden does just fine. But this wasn't the end of that story . . .

On November 24, 2004, Brenden and I headed to AI Dupont for a psychological evaluation to assess his cognitive, academic, social, and emotional functioning. It was interesting and yet slightly disappointing, but it did overall show he was making some progress. They did report that at times he seemed confused, even after things were repeated, and his responses were brief, and he gave up when he felt the task was difficult. The report stated that his overall cognitive scores were average, and that had been reported before on previous evaluations. With his language skills, it was noted that he scored high in understanding with reference to spoken language; however, his expressive skills put him in the fiftieth percentile. On listening to paragraphs, he struggled with the main idea and details, because he did not have the ability to inference and predict. He scored in the thirty-seventh percentile. He also demonstrated poor planning ability and problem-solving and organizational skills. He did tend to stick to only one way of solving a problem, even if it was faulty. The interesting piece was with his auditory attention. Here he scored in the low fifth percentile. He had significant difficulty responding to auditory information. He was disorganized, delayed in response and random in responses. So when assessing his academic functioning, it, again, showed that he struggled with higher order comprehension, for both the spoken and written word. Finally, the most interesting of all was the comparison of my rating him on attention and emotional function and the teacher ratings. I placed Brenden as struggling with attention, placed him very often having difficulty completing work, needing supervision to get through assignments, disorganized, and having trouble concentrating. I also noted that he struggled to develop steps to carry out a task and had difficulty beginning one. Now here is the interesting part. The teacher ratings yielded no significant findings. So, wow, just wow. Are we talking about two completely different children here? I mean this is a huge problem. No wonder they are not responsive. I am saying things they don't acknowledge as factual.

In the recommendation section, they did talk about his reading issues, stressing effort needed to be given to his critical thinking skills in the area of reading and writing, stating he needed in class support.

The report then talked about the need to care for his auditory system. It stated he should not be "overwhelmed by auditory input." It then gave me the parent strategies for reading at home. Honestly, I was already doing all that—preteaching, looking at pictures, asking *wh* questions, using Kidspirations. I felt that might help get his reading on grade level again, but remember the teacher had to implement the strategies, the one who rated his executive functioning as average, and I could not have disagreed more.

The school then completed their own psychological assessment. It took five days from January 21 to February 22. The IEP meeting was the next day. That's right, I got to read it on the fly or really not at all. I listened because only the teacher was involved in supplying information to the school psychologist about Brenden's social, emotional, and behavioral functioning. Guess what, she said he was average but did note his elevated anxiety. Interestingly, when the psychologist asked Brenden what he liked about himself, he stated, "Autism, from a different country, eat cheesesteaks." He then went on to say that he saw himself different from "normal" kids and that he cannot do "normal people work." The evaluator talked about how he needed to celebrate his differences but also knew he had things in common with other children. She talked about him needing a sense of belonging, instead of feeling alone. Sure, I thought that would be nice, but since he has very little social skills, how will that happen? He was alone. There was no one else like him in his class, and honestly, he knew it. She actually wrote, "The IEP team, which includes the parents, needs to determine an appropriate program for Brenden in the least restrictive setting that will meet his needs." I would love to, I thought. An appropriate program? I discussed that in the report, it stated I was a source of information and interviewed; this was incorrect. The meeting continued, and I was able to incorporate some of the outside evaluation findings into the present levels, but was amazed at wording such as "with receptive and expressive language skills being within normal limits." In reference to his auditory differences, they stated, "He demonstrated good attention to task and the ability to follow verbal instructions in the presence of auditory distractions." No sensory goals were added. He was placed on OT consult only once a month. Most of the goals on the IEP were referenced to his language issues, communication issues, and one goal about reading. At least there would be some movement there, and the special education teachers were in tune, and they would meet with the regular education teacher weekly to develop strategies. I had deep concerns about the reading issues. I was noticing that although he struggled with higher-level thinking, he also was skipping words, sometimes lines of words, and complaining of headaches all the time. I had multiple notes from the nurse about him needing Tylenol for a headache. I had him in vision therapy, and the doctor wrote to the school, but it was remarkably not recognized, and strategies recommended were not followed.

After the meeting, I went home to digest the report and all the information. The psychologist wrote in the report that Brenden had strange ideas. She talked about the rating scales, the ones I did not fill out, as useful information as it captures what caregivers see on a regular basis. What? I mean the teachers are being referred to as caregivers? I wrote a letter delivered the very next day to remove the report, as there were false statements or at the least misleading ones, and that I was not in fact interviewed as it stated in the report, nor did I complete any rating scales. I was told by the school that the report could not be revised. The psychologist did call me at home and discussed having me involved in the assessment, and I did then complete a rating scale as the caregiver. I just couldn't understand why as a member of the IEP team and as the parent my input was not requested. I, then, requested mediation on the issue, but the school ignored my request. I wrote the superintendent of schools, and they forwarded my request to the state. This was not a good time for us. I was struggling to get the school to follow procedural guidelines. So much time is wasted when this happens, and honestly, we were running out of time . . .

CHAPTER 14

GET HIM OUT OF THERE

There was an incident in class one day again, with the boy that was making faces at Brenden. In the past, I tried to explain to the teacher that this was causing Brenden great stress, and he was feeling overwhelmed with the situation, mostly because he did not understand it and what it meant. He didn't have the social skills to problem solve the issue with the boy. But there was no help from the teacher, and then one day, Brenden made a face back to the boy, and the teacher made an example of him in front of the entire class about making faces to others.

After school that day, we had vision therapy. He was quiet but handed me a note, which read, "Mom, I got my feelings hurt today. Love BC."

I asked him to tell me what happened. He said, after he made a face, the teacher yelled at him until he cried, and then she told him to stop crying and said, "I don't accept tears." I was infuriated,. He was so sad. He told me he couldn't go back. His anxiety was turning into fear. I wrote to the principal for support on the issue, and the response was that although the teacher's conduct was not appropriate, they don't discipline teachers for that. The teacher herself stated she was using a modeling technique with Brenden. I had no choice. I wanted to sit in that class myself to see exactly what went on. I did so for four days. I got to see that the easy reader or index card he was to use when reading was nowhere in the room. He read all morning like

78

that, and then it made sense why all the headaches. *I had written a letter to the team about his visual impairment, and so did the doctor.* At the beginning of the fourth day, I was asked to leave, and I was happy to go. I called Brenden over to his locker, and I said I had to go and asked him if he could stay by himself. He replied, "I want to go with you." I didn't know where we were going other than home, but soon fate would intervene, and we would find our safe place.

Brenden's Landscape

This was the most emotional year of my young life. My dad was in Iraq fighting for our country, and I was fighting for the right to be educated.

I didn't think school would be bad. I thought it would be like second grade. Nope. Old Yeller was something. Her facial expression and the way she presented her herself was scary.

I do recall the morning of a spring day in 2005. A day that would spur the process of me earning an appropriate education. The day where the educational reboot began. A day that decided my educational destiny.

Obviously, when my mom asked me if I wanted to go home with her when we stepped into the classroom, I said yes because I didn't want to go to school like any other kid at the time.

I do recall a blonde teacher who would come to my house from the end of April to June. I can remember crying when I said goodbye on the last day.

CHAPTER 15

HOME AND HOSPITAL

So panic kind of set in, but I was on a mission. First, I called the State Board of Education, I explained my situation, and I also made it known that Brenden could not return to the present environment. I was put in contact with a parent resource center that honestly made me feel like everything was going to be resolved, and they helped me make a plan. They told me Brenden could be homeschooled for the remainder of the year and that the district would supply the teacher if his doctor stated he would require a more restrictive environment. I was so relieved, and Brenden was as well, and although this was a temporary measure, it gave me and Brenden the time we needed to plan.

On April 19, 2005, the IEP team met to arrange for home and hospital teaching placement. (HHT). I remember feeling so calm during this meeting. The struggles would be over. This was one tumultuous year. The plan was for Brenden to return to a school-based program, but the writing was on the wall for me. We had to start looking at schools that had our vision. This was not the school. Brenden was feeling stressed, worried, and frustrated about being at this school, in particular this grade and this teacher. So for seven weeks, six hours a week (three days, two hours per day), things were at peace. Brenden developed such a great relationship with the home-based teacher. He felt so comfortable with her that he communicated his feelings, asked for breaks, and told her when he was feeling frustrated. The teacher did note that writing was difficult for Brenden, and without the one-on-one attention, he would not have been successful. When the teacher left at the end of the sessions, Brenden cried and said, "I want you. I need you. I love you with all my heart." He was kind of into Elvis then, so to him, the song had meaning. He was so sincere, but this woman gave him peace of mind, and he connected to her. I'll never forget it.

While Brenden was learning and succeeding and feeling good about his progress, I was waiting for mediation. I just couldn't have a repeat of third grade. On the days that Brenden didn't have a teacher come to the house, I was calling many schools in PA. I asked if I could tour their school, I asked if they had children on the spectrum. I asked if they believed in inclusion. You would be surprised, but many schools told me I couldn't tour, that I would disrupt the class schedules and the students. I found that to be a sign. There is probably something they don't want me to see, or perhaps they can't handle our situation. But there was one school in Pennsylvania. Yes, there was, and it had vision, and the principal at the time believed in that vision. She toured us around the school. It was three times the size of the current school. But we were not overwhelmed; we were content, and as we walked through this one schoolhouse, I noticed that they had computers and that a child was using Kidspirations. When I tell you that we then met two influential teachers who would touch our lives in such a way that forever we were changed for good. The principal promoted inclusion, and she delivered it daily, along with the staff. It is so true that with great leadership at the top, there is greatness all around. She told me if I was coming to the district to do it soon, I intended to waste no time. I saw the miracles around me that day, and now I set my mind to making this dream become a reality.

Mediation finally occurred on May 9, and I participated because to me it would be final then, and I had things to say. I have to say that mediation is exactly what it says, and if attorneys were not there, I believe the parents and the district could work things out better together, in the small-group situation. I went alone. This was my last hurrah so to speak. I was nervous but not afraid. I wanted to make a point especially concerning the evaluation that did not include me.

The school was saying that they did not have to include me. How does that make a valid assessment? The IEP team should include the parent as a member, and if the school you're in does not respect you as a team member, you're in the wrong school. Actually, as the parent, you should be able to have input and advocate for your child's education and not have your rights ignored. In this school, every discipline functioned on their own, not as a team in my opinion. For example, if there was a speech and language goal, that should carry over into the classroom, not just while the student is at speech. Goals need to be measurable and show progress. I like short-term or benchmark goals, with data to back up the growth. Here is an unmeasurable goal: Brenden will understand pragmatic language 100 percent of the time. Here is a measurable goal: Brenden will reciprocate understanding of social conversation evidenced by his ability to have two volleys of conversation at recess and when in small group.

I wasn't asking for much; so I sat with three members of the IEP team, an attorney representing the school, and the mediator, who was impartial. The entire meeting I also knew that Brenden was not going back there, not ever. Our house was on the market, and I knew it would sell. We were making plans, but, first, I had to know if what I was currently asking of the school was appropriate. I thought it was, but I was learning by doing, not always the best position to be in. During the meeting, I do recall yelling coming from me. I didn't care for the school attorney, at all. I should've handled it better. The mediator was my lifeline. I was done. At the end of the meeting, there was a settlement. The psychological assessment would be revised to remove me as part of the sources of information. The caregivers in the report were the educators, and it should read as such. Last, the words about Brenden hearing voices would be removed. The report would stay as a part of his record. In reference to Brenden's sensory issues, an adaptive PE teacher, an OT, and a regular education teacher would prepare a plan so he could participate in physical education. Brenden would receive psychological services proposed at an earlier IEP meeting from March. That was never incorporated. This would include collecting data on his social functioning.

There was a follow-up IEP meeting in June, and as I sat there full well knowing he would not be returning to this school, I had a sense for the very first time of how things should have been all along. Why was this so hard? Why has an entire year been spent on waiting for them to get this? When I heard statements like these being said, "Provide a place for Brenden to go when he feels stressed," "Use of earplugs during PE class, deep-pressure activities such as wall push-ups, use of the therapy ball, repetitive pictures for understanding directions," "Limit activities that require touching, and use written words if he is overwhelmed," all these and then some on the IEP, I was vindicated, I was advocating, and Brenden and I were about to embark on the best years of our lives.

Brenden's Landscape

Looking back, that day started a train of events that would change my fate.

I do recall the day my mom and I toured the new school. I being welcomed by Mrs. Barry, the principal at the time. She welcomed me and my mom with a huge smile.

CHAPTER 16

THE BIG EASY

When we moved, Brenden made these statements about himself: "It's my autism that makes me think wrong," and "I am stupid." He described his disability of autism as like having kid Alzheimer's. Everything was weighing heavily on his mind, but we were starting over, and we had to do this for him as a family. I was so very lucky to have my family's help at this time, because the house we bought was in need of a transformation. The market was tight, meaning there were not a lot of homes in this district in our price range. But we found an older home, and I will never forget the day of settlement. When we arrived, the house looked like it had been abandoned. The backyard was so overgrown you would need a machete to walk through it! My mom was with the kids, and settlement was right down the street. The owner would not be there, as she was on vacation. I thought this would be easy as pie. We were there for four hours. It was a series of events, and when we got home, I saw my mom lying on the cat-pee-stained blue carpets, moaning about her back. She was in pain, and now we had to get her back to her place. The kids looked like they were going to cry, but help was on the way. The very next day, as we awoke to the mushroom farm smell that we were not prepared for, the troops arrived, and we pulled up that carpet and cleaned. Another miracle around us. I would not have survived it. It was over-whelming. You cannot thank your family enough for these things, and especially my sister, who managed to give me a much-needed foot rub. I have not one but two Theresas, and that pretty much has covered me all my life.

Luckily, I had the summer to organize and get the kids registered for school. Brenden would be starting fourth-grade and Emily half-day kindergarten. I know Brenden was nervous, but he honestly had the best teachers he could hope for. It was an inclusion class, with a regular education teacher and a special education teacher who pushed in. In other words, Brenden would not be pulled for instruction. There was also a wonderful autistic support special education teacher who was his case manager. Barb truly gave her all to every student, but for Brenden, she was a true advocate. The fourth-grade teachers. Helena and Jeff were awesome together in class. Like peanut butter is to jelly or the cheese to the macaroni, yep, just like that. Over and beyond educating Brenden, they actually made him feel as if he could do anything. It was a true model of inclusion, with the supports necessary to pull out all the strengths hiding inside him. Up till now, only weaknesses had been addressed. It almost made Brenden seem like he was not living, but here in the fourth grade, a huge transformation took place. I am not saying he didn't struggle at times, because he did. The difference was he was guided to handle things a whole lot better. He was learning to be a part of a community of learners and people. He was trying to navigate the social world.

I used to focus so much on the academic portion of his IEP, so much that when I finally experienced what an appropriate education looked like and felt like, I really learned about progressing. In the past, when I had struggled to reach educators about teaching a child with autism, I was speaking my own language. Everything I talked about—my insight, my emotion, my knowledge—none of this had an impact. They were clueless, not on purpose; it just wasn't familiar. There was no awareness. I could remember saying in a meeting at our old school, "I don't even know what his strengths are?" Did I know? Of course I did, but I was so distracted with helping him read or interpret abstract math problems that I forgot about his ability. Brenden had great strengths, his memory, and his determination to complete what was asked of him. He was motivated and had great ideas and loved to invent things. Now I was getting to see how to motivate and engage Brenden to learn as part of this class. Progress, of course, it can be a struggle, but all of us struggle with things. Kids with autism are no different. His strength in geometry always fascinated me. It's like visualizing three dimensions was something he did all the time. He didn't even need to think about it. Fractions were difficult too abstract, but with pictures or visuals, I saw that he could understand. Reading was also a challenge due to difficulty with the higher meaning of the story or theory of mind. Most of the time, he could remember details and characters, and even breakdown what happens in the beginning middle and end of the story. It always seemed to be a problem to figure out why or to predict guessing was too abstract but not beyond his ability. For example, you know when you see someone standing too close to the edge of something, and you realize they will probably fall off. Someone with autism has to have this literally pointed out to them. We can understand it. Some people call it intuition. Seeing the big picture is essential to getting along in all walks of life. Brenden amazed me, though, in that he always could sense who was a kind person or, in his words, "pretty in their heart." According to him, that is what is important. Talk about insight.

I could talk about all the wonderful things about fourth grade, and that would be a book in itself, but the biggest thing to me was the Black History Performance. In February of that year, with hives and all, Brenden insisted, "I can do it." Part of the play included the class signing to the song "What Wonderful World." He was comfortable with that, and I think it helped him fit in. He also had other parts in the performance, but he never told me about the dancing! He was wonderful! He seemed to take forever to get his hat and gloves on, but everyone waited for him, and not impatiently. This class took the lead from the wonderful teachers that everyone was accepted, not judged for their differences. This made Brenden be the best he could be; he was comfortable. If everyone lived by this example, all would live life to their potential. You see, life skills are just as important as an education, and I was starting to see him have a life and be like his peers, something he always hoped for. So there he was dancing away. He looked scared to death, but he was succeeding! Then the fire alarm went off. It was so loud! I never knew it was that loud! There was no time to prepare him, of course, no time for earplugs, so when I saw him in the parking lot, he was bursting into tears. He wouldn't let go of me. He was so upset; but there was Helena to the rescue, giving him praise and encouragement, refocusing him, and getting him ready to begin again. I couldn't have been more proud of Brenden that night. He rallied to finish the performance. Helena also had it taped and gave each parent a copy. I will treasure that night forever and can look back on the memories anytime. The best part would have to be that I had no idea how this would go, and the teachers involved never told me a thing. They let me be surprised with that dance routine, Brenden and his two flappers. It was an *Aha!* moment, let me tell you. I never saw that coming, and I didn't need to worry because he was in the best hands. The world can be cruel, and some think the word *disability* means no ability, but all it is, is a disadvantage. Here in fourth grade, it was all about being given a chance, and it set the stage for two more years of growth and celebration of spreading of awareness.

As with all things, It wasn't always sunshine and roses for Brenden, because at times his behavior took over, and he found himself in situations. Like all kids at this age, growing up and controlling your emotions is challenging. Physical education was a time of great frustration for him. He liked sports but just couldn't play them that well. They had a PT evaluation done on him, which was very telling. With a point score of 0/15 in the area of running speed and agility, he scored a 1. He was below average with balance, low with bilateral coordination and strength. The therapist stated that he was eager to perform and tried hard to succeed, but the limitations would require some therapy. So we all agreed to thirty minutes a week direct PT. I will never forget his PE teacher Stacy Mengal. She truly had Brenden's best interests at heart, and she was able to involve him in games and be supportive.

One day, his emotions got the best of him in there, and I suppose in anger, he pushed her; he pushed his teacher! I was working there as a paraprofessional in autistic support, so she brought him down at the end of the day so we could talk it out. I really admired her for that. She didn't owe that to me or to him. She was kind. I was worried. I never had seen him do something like that, this kind of mistake you have to sleep on. There would be consequences, of course, but I wanted to see him be remorseful, and he was. That is so important that they understand the seriousness of their actions. I know to this day Brenden will not forget it, but he could be forgiven so that he could move past it. So very thankful for that!

At the same time, an OT evaluation was being done. Ms. Trish was no doubt one of the best therapists Brenden has had. Based on testing, she picked up the visual and motor deficits, which were affecting his ability to copy information with speed. She also noted his extreme difficulties processing sensory information throughout his school day. Motor planning came up along with body aware-ness. He had great difficulty completing bilateral hand coordination activities. His letter formation was big, and when he drew a person, the arms and legs were not in proportion with the body. She recom-mended many things, one was earplugs for the gym and lunch and use of an easy reader to highlight the words on the line he was read-ing. Sensory breaks were built into his day. I often remember seeing him in the hall walking or pitching a fake baseball. She also worked on a program with him called How Does Your Engine Run. It is an alert program that teaches self-regulation, as it compares to how a car runs and tries to teach the child with sensory dysfunction to change their level of alertness for the situation they are in. They learn to identify their engine "speed" like a car, low, high, or just right. They used pictures to show what low, high, and just right looked like. In my opinion, it really did help Brenden work on self-regulation, and in his words, "At least it isn't a frog, like in Kelso's choices, because everyone knows frogs can't talk!"

I had consented to a reevaluation by the school psychologist upon arrival to update his educational needs. He was not in need of a speech reevaluation, so he just received speech therapy three times a week for thirty minutes for problem-solving and metalinguistic skills. This is basically the ability to identify language and under-stand what it means. He really needed leading questions or cues to use higher-order thinking, not to mention pragmatic and life skills.

He was able to recognize the problem or issue but unable to explain or rectify the situation. I was asked to provide a parent narrative:

Brenden is very happy to be at this new school. We, as a family, had a terrible third-grade experience. Our last school lacked education and supports to appropriately educate Brenden. His anxiety was severe toward the end of third grade. He was under doctor's care and homeschooled for the last seven weeks of school. Even though this helped him, this was not what I wanted for him. He turned again to his "aloneness." Brenden's friends are few but supportive. He is very open about his autism and quite knowledgeable. His biggest problems are communication, and often his "words" are misread or misinterpreted. He has worked really hard with social skills and completed behavior classes. He still struggles but needs this so badly. His life skills are not good. I know he relies on me for a lot, but I have always been there to help him along. Advocating for Brenden became a full-time job for me but not a burden. He is a joy to have around, and his different ways of thinking often teach me. Brenden's dad was away for fourteen months serving in Iraq. This was very difficult for him. His sister, Emily, is very supportive, and if not for her, sometimes, I think he would not participate in anything. She shows him and tells him often what to do and how to act unconditionally. She is a gem! We moved here because we believe the school embraces true inclusion. We saw this personally, and now that we are here, we already know things are and will get better for Brenden.

In fifth and sixth grade, there were multiage classes. It was really a great way to teach. The mixture of the fifth and sixth grade really helped socially. Along again a great team of teachers, Mr. Murray and Mrs. Flood, we were so lucky to have them all. Brenden's teacher Mr. Murray also liked the same football team he did, the Fighting Irish of Notre Dame. That rarely happens, but it did, and Brenden even received a letter from coach Kelly, after Mr. Murray wrote him about Brenden being a fan of the team. He still keeps it framed in his room. That moment was priceless. One of the most awesome things was the class all connected to pen pals from Italy. Brenden received Andrea Ghignone's name. They have remained friends till this day. They have shared their love of music and have exchanged gifts. Brenden hopes one day to actually meet him in person. I hope he can. I pray he does.

During the last years, Brenden's case manager, Barb, had asked both Brenden and me to speak about autism and to help spread awareness. We saw it as an opportunity to give back. I also always felt like helping classmates and teachers alike understand his perspective. Soon everyone would invariably accept him. We always did interactive presentations and always had plenty of people to help us. We talked about sensory challenges so others could actually feel the anxiety and the panic with events that ordinarily wouldn't phase them. For example, we would start with a teacher rushing into the room, telling everyone to clear their desk. She would announce a pop spelling quiz that had to be done now, per administration. She then called out, "Get a pencil, a piece of paper." All the while someone was flickering the lights on and off, and someone was banging a cowbell! Meanwhile, the teacher is calling out words that were impossible to spell, and she would not even give them time to write it or ask a question. As I looked around the room, the kids were all so confused. Some didn't even have paper out! It was great to start with this activity because it showed everyone how someone with autism would feel with all the sensory overload.

Another activity we did just for teachers was about how using visual strategies was key for someone on the spectrum. There was a woman who spoke French, Mrs. Duvall, and worked with us on this. I asked her to give the directions to the staff on how to set a table but not in English; it had to be in French. There were specific directions like place the blue cup on the right hand side of the plate and put the napkin under the fork. We had them attempt to set the table twice, once with just verbal directions and another with verbal direction and a picture of the table setting to help them. The impact was great. I could feel their frustration as they tried so hard to understand the foreign words and then see their relief when they had the picture. It was just like a thousand words.

In sixth grade, Brenden again was having visual difficulties, and the teachers were reporting that he was reading two grade levels below what he should be. It seemed to be his inability to answer inferential questions. However, the visual impairments that he had to deal with were ever present, and I felt that they were directly impacting his progress. He definitely had visual stress, and even though he continued every year in visual therapy outside of school, I felt that he needed some in-school accommodations. Brenden had started to request books on tape. He knew that his hearing was his strength when his vision was altered. Brenden had a great work ethic. I cannot tell you how important it is to instill that early on and look for accommodations over modifications; there is a huge difference. Brenden also was requesting to tape his journal responses. He struggled with writing, especially at night after a long day at school. I felt this would also increase his independence along with his self-esteem, because he could then complete things on his own. Things took time, but the support he had in this school was wonderful! The expectation of what he could accomplish was amazing. This was a team. So the team decided to look outside the school walls to the local Intermediate Unit. Here we requested a Functional Vision Evaluation. All I needed was a script from his eye doctor stating that he needed the eval for reading and computer work. A binocular visual processing evaluation.

The evaluation was key to Brenden's motivation to finally rise above this frustrating problem. For years, he struggled to read because words were moving on a page, headaches, plain old visual impairment! His teachers in school had started enlarging his print material to see if his grades and performance improved. The larger text eased the stress for him immediately. He had a significant history of convergence insufficiency. He had been in visual therapy for years, and although motivated in each session, the problems resurfaced over and over. Some of the evaluation methods that I found interesting were that they used a word search puzzle where he could only find three out of the ten words. This deals with scanning. Brenden basically gave up because he was too difficult for him and that the words were moving on the page. For tracking, he had to read letters at sixteen-point font. He lost his place from left to right and incorrectly read sixteen out of the twenty-three lines of text. He skipped letters, reversed them, skipped entire rows, and inserted letters. Brenden commented that if he saw two letters, his eyes made him read four. Interestingly enough he could scan a document for numbers, and was able to slow down his speed when told to locate them. With his reading speed, it was found that he struggled to read the text that had twelve-to-fourteen-point font. When he received an eighteen-point font, his speed and accuracy improved greatly. For his visual discrimination, he scored poorly on the six out of seven subtests. For example, he incorrectly identified the word *umb* for *bun*, the word *guns* for *sung*, *on* for *no*. Imagine trying to read to learn when you're not even reading the correct words.

They actually also gave him a math test, one in ten-point font, the other in twenty-point font. The results showed that his speed and accuracy improved greatly with use of large print materials. While using trials of magnification, he also read with less errors and stress while reading. His was also greatly motivated by his increased reading scores while using the magnifier or enlarged font. This was key for me to read myself. Being motivated would surely increase how he learns and help him progress.

Due to that evaluation, he did qualify for vision support services. His difficulty functioning in the classroom was soon to improve through the use of enlarged print materials and accommodations. In the recommendations, it noted that when reading Brenden struggled with materials that were smaller than twenty-four-point font, but his accuracy and reading speed were affected if it was smaller than thirty-six-point font. Nevertheless, out of this evaluation came to be a trial for assistive technology devices to assist in viewing materials and using books on tape for reading materials. Funny to even say books on tape now, but back in 2008, that was what would save him and give his taxed visual system a break. There were not a lot of kids that needed these services at the time, and making his materials in the correct font was a little tricky. The vision teacher would ask for materials from the classroom teachers a week in advance so that she could enlarge the papers and bring them back. He also got to use a CCTV, which would enlarge textbooks by magnifying it onto a screen. The trouble was you had to keep moving the book because it would cut words off, and it was huge, not portable at all. But beyond the obstacles, things got better for him, and his reading improved.

I used to think all the time he was in vision therapy, no one mentioned enlarged print, wondering whether his convergence/accommodative disorder would go away or not. His headaches lessened, and honestly, he was less frustrated with reading with enlarged print. His self-esteem improved, and frankly, he was more comfortable with the thirty-six-point font. This was hard to accomplish, and some of the copies of papers were copied so many times and not the original, so they were lighter. Technology was coming, though, and in the end, it was the solution, but it was the end of sixth grade; he was going to the middle school next.

Brenden started a trial use of a laptop for the use of speech recognition software. The program was called Dragon Naturally Speaking. Brenden did have difficulty with writing, and the team felt he could benefit from this program. He couldn't type well. It had to be managed with OT. It was like hunt and peck, and loud! They were so spot-on he took to this program without hesitation. He learned all the commands and prompts to be successful. He would even say it to anyone today that Dragon gave him the ability to write. It was amazing he would need to process his thoughts, but then all he had to do was talk. All those years without words, and here he was using his words! Everything was getting better for him, but it was a time of transition. We were hesitant, and we really had no clue how hard the next year would turn out to be.

CHAPTER 17

MISTAKES, I MADE A FEW

Middle school, we were not prepared, not in any shape or form. It was like being in a fishbowl. No one was keenly aware of anything he needed to be successful, and there he was, just swimming, everyone watching. From the beginning, I made many mistakes. I wrote my first complaint to the Department of Education, since we had been in the district since fourth grade. I was not successful. I was fighting so hard that I lost sight of my emotions. I was reacting instead of thinking. I was not being very effective. We were new to this school, and the autistic support teacher was new as well, brand-new. This created an environment that was extremely stressful for Brenden, and his frustration was mounting. The warning signs actually started over the summer, when we received a letter that because of his PSSA Reading scores he would have to take a course called Strategic Reading. The principal called this an opportunity, as it would pro-vide direct instruction and support necessary to improve his reading skills. So he could receive this "opportunity," he would have to miss taking art cycle classes. He would miss exploratory French, Spanish, and music. In the second half of the year, he would miss life studies to attend literacy enrichment. I called the principal because I wanted him to understand that Brenden was not a standardized test result he was a student. I informed him that Brenden had been reading *French for Dummies* to prepare for class, because he was that motivated. He politically stated that he loved when he heard that about a student.

I thought, *Great, he gets how important this is.* It didn't matter. He said he was responsible for making sure Brenden was ready for high school. Actually, I thought I was.

I requested to talk with the director of special education who informed me that placement in this class was separate from the IEP. This was the criteria for all seventh- and eighth-grade students, regardless. I was confused. He was to be in cotaught classes for support. How would this work? Was this class even research based? I had never heard of it. I was so angry and apprehensive at the same time. I was scrambling, confused, and feeling very unsure of what I was doing. This is not a good place to be.

That angry part, try not to be that person, even if it's all you can do to hold it together. This strategic reading program had no research basis. It was just something the school instituted to increase the scores on the state assessment the PSSA. I pleaded and was relentless with this principal. Brenden spent one semester in that class, and the principal agreed that he could be removed if he scored proficient in his 4Sight reading assessment. And that he did. Was it because of that class? Not possible, because the very next 4Sight test the next semester, he was advanced in reading. He never had to do that again, and for that, I would say continue to seek out the most appropriate education, because that word *appropriate* gets lost in the shuffle of test scores and the bottom line. This quote became a favorite one of mine that I often thought should be read prior to every IEP meeting. It was written by Haim Ginott.

> I possess tremendous power to make a child's life miserable or joyous. I can be a tool of torture or an instrument of inspiration. I can humiliate or humor, hurt or heal. In all situations it is my response that decides whether a crisis will be escalated or de-escalated, and a child humanized or dehumanized.

In about a month, Brenden was due for his three-year reevaluation, and at the time, I was asked for my input. I said, "Brenden is autistic, but more important is, he likes how he is." He often tells me he is not interested in recovery as others he has met. Building his self-esteem is as important as building his self-advocacy skills. I went on to say, "He now has voice-activated software on his laptop that has given him so much needed independence from the task of writing his responses. He clearly has emerging skills here, and now that his visual needs are recognized, I feel he will improve in all areas of information." I stated his strengths were that he was motivated, worked hard, and was respectful and kind to others. His view of things was always different and yet true. I also stated that he was making new friends but was never invited to anything. His needs were great with his sensory system, especially when in PE class. I also admired him for the person he was and the person he was striving to be. Brenden did try to spread awareness with his classmates, teachers, and others. He did not shy away from having autism. It was a part of him.

Brenden still needed much support at the school, OT, speech and vision support. But the one guy who helped the most was the one guy we never saw coming. There was a lot of help from the CCIU. Things were not working the best they could with just having teachers enlarge the print for him. Often, things were not prepared ahead of time, and Brenden would just have to do without his enlarged print materials. There were incidents of tests not being in the correct font, and Brenden went to his case manager for help, yet still he was told to take the test. No one went to enlarge it. It wasn't that the staff had no idea how or what to do. The vision teacher met with the staff at the beginning of the year and provided a snapshot for them of his needs. It was also on his SDI section of the IEP (Specially Designed Instruction). They even typed an example of what he needed to be successful, and when I think he had to read all day, I can't even imagine Brenden's frustration! The teachers had no time to do it. Let's be honest. Who knows what the situation was? He had some very dedicated teachers, but things are different in middle school; you have many teachers. There was a production clerk that if the materials were submitted ahead of time, they would be ready. We hired an advocate, because honestly, I was feeling like I was being thrown under the bus. I thought we worked as a team. I tried to ask the special education coordinator to help the staff. It wasn't going to happen. I will never regret the decision to seek additional help. I took the recommendation from a support group I was a member of. This woman was the best. She got things done, even when she merely showed up at the meeting. It was costly but worth every penny. She reviewed his records, and she guided me. She never spoke for me unless I was yelling, and indeed I did. Not proud of that, but I was again a little ignorant to how things could be so different from one school to another in the same district. She empowered me and taught me how to avoid or resolve conflict. She made it possible to work out a meaningful plan so Brenden could be educated. It was in fact what Brenden needed, and as simple as that was to me, it was not automatically to others.

I felt that his vision teacher Kory summed up what Brenden's visual needs were the best when she did a review of records. She wrote convergence insufficiency is a common condition that is characterized by a person's inability to maintain proper binocular eye alignment on objects as they approach from distant to near. The symptoms associated with an accommodative disorder related to prolonged visually demanding center tasks may include headaches, visual fatigue, and/or eye strain. A deficiency of the saccades is a fairly common eye problem in which people are unable to follow a moving object accurately or unable to shift their eyes from one point of fixation to another. The deficiency of pursuits means that Brenden has difficulty smoothly tracking an object. Lastly, a visual motor developmental delay means that Brenden lacks the ability to coordinate the motor movement with visual stimulus. So in short terms, he was having trouble with what he was seeing and then following that up with a motor response. For example, copying from the blackboard or shooting a ball into the basket.

Socially, this year was a complete disaster for Brenden as well. With the new autistic support teacher in the building, things did not appear to be individualized but mostly group oriented. It also didn't help that there was really only one class period that could be used for social skill instruction for everyone in that grade. With that in mind, it appeared that anyone on the spectrum regardless of your social skill need was placed into the same group. So, for example, if they were working on teaching the skill of turn taking, you were in that group regardless of the fact that you already had mastered that. This completely sent Brenden into a tailspin. He had been in groups like this outside of school and could not handle being told to do things he already knew how to do. He could not relate to this being helpful, but this was the reality. There were meetings about this issue, and many people were involved, but ultimately, he had to be removed from the large group social skills assignment because it was inappropriate. For the most part, the CCIU helped again by working to develop a program with the social skill needs that would be identified for Brenden. However, this is an issue that falls short in many schools. Schools need a mentor program that helps develop appropriate social skills. Sitting in a room full of kids with weaknesses does not build strength. It also isolates them and keeps them from engaging in activities other kids their age are doing. There just has to be a better way to deliver this service in real time so that the kids can benefit and learn. It most certainly is a huge consideration when picking a school, because beyond academics, social issues are the true test of your young middle schooler. Brenden would write down what he did during his social skills classes. He wrote, "People are running around. It was loud," "We had to make a puzzle of the US without talking, using our body language," "I took a puzzle piece out of Luis's hand, but I didn't mean it. I am great at history, and Michigan is not near Florida," "I was just trying to help." He went on to say how the people in social skills act. They scream, call out, they are hyper, they never stop talking, they are touchy. He referred to middle school as a "stress causer that strengthens anger."

Brenden had unique needs that needed to be planned for. In reference to reading, writing, and enlarging text and font size, there were issues with when and how to let him use the voice recognition technology. On his SDI (specifically designed instruction), it stated he could write up to four sentences in the classroom, but if he requested, he could just use his technology. He had to usually go into the hallway, and although not ideal, it worked for the most part. The teachers were trying, but his visual fatigue was greater as the day went on. It was becoming clear that he would need more visual strategies to progress. For example, he preferred the font to be thirty-six; but that created some issues, with the flow of certain documents, and frustration for Brenden to read across the page. The visual support team recommended a larger laptop of seventeen inches to facilitate that, along with more software like Kurzweil, Adobe, and Zoom text. That would cover the technical needs, but the need for things to get done were strangled. There needed to be a point of contact in the building to get things done. Only having a production person was not good enough. The district would make a decision by the end of the seventh grade, which, in the future years, would cause much confrontation. The IEP team made a decision to disseminate a one to one aide. It was stated as follows on the IEP. Adult support for vision support, scribing, production, and enlarging. Assistive technology available to Brenden as first priority. Under the present levels, I had this added to the IEP. I believed that the present levels should state exactly what the student looks like so that everyone could read that and understand how the student functioned. It read like this.

With the use of a laptop and voice recognition for use at home and school due to the difficulty visualizing the keyboard and inability to type with speed and accuracy, voice-activated software is used to allow him to be independent. His open-ended responses are then independently dictated in math, science, social studies, and language arts. By reducing the amount of writing tasks, Brenden exhibits less frustration. This has made a significant difference in Brenden's academic performance.

I also felt as if there was school-wide confusion about the definition of *modification* versus *accommodations*. Brenden had only accommodations in that he was not having anything modified in what he was expected to learn. There was no change in his curriculum, just that he received teaching support or a service. Using technology was indeed an accommodation. My advice, give attention to the wording of things, be an integral part of the IEP team, and above all involve your child as soon as you feel they are ready. Baby steps, indeed, but advocating is a skill. Self-advocating needs to be taught and encouraged, and to be totally honest, the team members understand a lot better when the information is coming from the person everyone is sitting around the table planning for. When Brenden said something, it usually made sense, and it was profound. It actually made him more flexible to new ideas if he was part of the decision-making process.

By eighth grade, things were running more smoothly. There were regular meetings, and issues were discussed, and the planning continued. The classrooms all had scanners, and Brenden was trialing digital formats of papers. With the aide in place, Brenden was able to access things in class that were not scanned in prior or if the teacher changed or added things. Except for math, that was easier if it remained a pencil and paper area, and this remained consistent through the years. Brenden was improving both academically and somewhat socially. With the use of technology, he was receiving high honors. At the end of the middle school years, Brenden had become more of a success. Sadly, the aide who worked with him would not accompany him to the high school. He had become very close with her but understood that she needed to stay at the school. It was time for the final years, time for the critical years. Brenden wanted to go to college for broadcast journalism, and that was going to happen, but that forecast was at times unpredictable.

Prior to the end of eighth grade, we requested mediation to define the use of, and in fact the meaning of, what *one–one* would mean in reference to Brenden's needs. In an IEP meeting at the end of the school year, it became apparent the head of special education was not planning for the same assistance at the high school that was instituted at the middle school. I was clarifying what and specifically who would be the one–one support, and she told me that was not what one–one meant. There and then, I knew the true meaning of *discombobulated*! What? I started to think I was again the last one to know. *One-one*, I thought it was clear as day. Nope, not at all, and this had to be dealt with, so I thought, why not some mediation here? We needed to reach an agreement with someone who was impartial. The whole goal of mediation is mutual satisfaction, so I filed. In July of that summer, Brenden and I went to the meeting with the goal of having a binding agreement, and that is exactly what occurred. In fact, many things were easily resolved because of a third party. You do have to agree that the meeting will remain confidential, and anything said could not be used in a due process or any court proceedings. That was totally acceptable to me and Brenden. In fact, that meeting was quick and painless. It was clear that the focus was on getting things worked out for the benefit of the student. The one-to-one support was clearly defined in the agreement to be a designated person and placed in the SDI section of the IEP. We were also able to negotiate the completion of the Assessment of Basic Social Skills to make proper goals for Brenden as he entered high school. This assessment told us what skills he had as fundamentals and which skills were emerging. All members of the team, including myself and Brenden, completed this. I highly recommend using this because it can be done again to see progress or lack thereof. It is an excellent guide to teaching individualized social skills.

Brenden's Landscape

First Impression

My seventh-grade year was a disaster. I was just starting to adjust my curriculum because of larger font, and there was a lack of communication between my teachers and me.

Middle School Seventh grade. Worst year ever. It's a year I want to forget. I was dealing with typical middle school adjustment. The deeper social pool was a challenge diving into. I wasn't an athlete like most guys my age. I wasn't in band, theatre, robotics. It was just me on my own pool float drifting into the way of the pool current.

In the middle of that year, I was introduced to my assistive technology teacher, Mr. Brian McHugh from the Chester County Intermediate Unit. My first impression of him came with the thoughts of "Who the heck are you, and what will you do to help me?" Also, I would get annoyed inside when he came in to work with me at first. At that time, I was just ready for seventh grade to be done.

The following year, I began to use my seventeen-inch laptop to view my schoolwork and books. With this learning adjustment, Mr. McHugh made more frequent visits to train me. These sessions with him in eighth grade made me become more welcoming and to value him more. He trained me to use an iPad in my freshman year and useful apps such as AudioNote, GoodReader, and Read2Go, to name a few. He also trained me to use Dropbox in my sophomore, which has made my academic life revolve around it.

Ever since then, my relationship with him has changed. I now see him as a valuable resource for guidance on my technology and life in general. He also showed me programs that made me successful during my high school years. His contributions have changed my life because of me using assistive technology. I feel prepared for college and beyond because of him. Without him, I don't know where I'll be and how my life would have went.

I can in eighth grade say that the future starts now. Eighth grade was the true first step for me to get ready for college.

Eighth grade was one of my best school years. Teachers were on board. I was making friends, and accommodations were being met.

CHAPTER 18

THE FINAL FOUR

Brenden's Landscape

Goals List for High School
1. *Make friends.*
2. *Read more.*
3. *Try to ask a girl to a dance or a date.*
4. *Continue academic success and achievements.*
5. *Continue doing the morning announcements.*
6. *Take it one day at a time.*

I liked this list of goals, and let me state how important it is to make them. Clearly, without self-motivation, there can be no growth, nothing to look forward to no matter where your child receives his education. Brenden was working toward something, and he had quite a different outlook on things for sure. My favorite idea of his to become more social was his daily plan to sit somewhere new every day at lunch so he could meet new people. I thought it was brave, and I know that had to take courage to do, but he was self-motivating his day to day. The next four years would be interesting and not without some drama, but this was his future, and we had to get this done right. We were unsure of what would be, and it most certainly was unpredictable at times. This was difficult for him. But there was joy, and he grew from that joy and moved past the pain. In other words, this is life. Disability or not, you move forward, slowly inching your way to your ultimate goals and dreams. Brenden wanted to be college bound, and this was that final frontier. It was all about determination and a little help from some great teachers, and perhaps not-so-great teachers. Life is what you make of it, never giving up. We never did. There are no guarantees in life, but you go on.

Brenden's landscape

However, there is always one good thing taken from every bad experience. The only story worthy to be told is a man I met whose presence would make me become independent and a college-bound student.

Mr. Brian McHugh. A man who was a second father to me. I went from despising him to looking forward to seeing him every Monday during "Academic Learning Center" period.

I took psychology in my senior year of high school and the assignment about first impressions. I had to write about someone who I did not have a good first impression with but made a difference in my life.

There were early signs that maybe things at the high school may not be what we expected. Like the social skills program. It was called society skills, but the only society in there were other kids with disabilities. In hindsight, maybe it was a scheduling conflict. Maybe no one thought out of the box, but again, just as in middle school, Brenden and I didn't want to do this again. I really wanted a program-modeling mentor programs, something that would help someone like Brenden fit into society, not be packed away in a room away from society. I mean think about the message being sent, think about the friendship factor. My strongest emotions were how to change perceptions of knowing someone, who is just different, and accepting them into your group. Tolerance was missing, and again, we strived to at least pick our battles.

We decided that Brenden would just have social skills in his classroom, and we worked with teachers and his speech therapist on goals, like initiating skills to ask friends to hang out. He would reflect on experiences, and the teachers or therapists would record his thoughts. His one teacher thought he should write them himself, but writing did not help Brenden. It frustrated him. There were great moments for him, like getting invited to a sweet sixteen birthday party. There were other times when he invited kids to our house, only to have only one friend arrive. Thank you, Kyle Lewis, and it was fine you didn't like my sandwiches, but I knew it was a matter of time till you did. Brenden was lucky in life to have awesome cousins who showed up and made something horrible into a great day. When they drove down the street, my heart loved them more; it was beautiful.

I remember when Brenden was born, I gave all the cousins a book about adoption. We had great cousins all around, so supportive. My niece Kelly recently reminded me of what I wrote in the book to her and her brother:

> I give this book to you so you can understand how Brenden became part of our special family the Currys. He is loved by all of us, and he loves you both. Brenden will always have two moms. That's what makes him so special. He also has two special cousins. He is very blessed. Always try to help Brenden understand this, he will need your help especially as he gets older and realizes he is "different." I'm counting on you both!

Having a mentor across all environments in high school was what we were looking for, but it never transpired. He had a goal on his IEP that he would improve his social skills, exactly pretty broad—in fact, almost unmeasurable. However, Brenden seemed to be able to rise above it, and he was mostly drawn to older students, so I guess you could say he found his own mentors. I have to admire that in him. What great courage he must have had to forge on every day. It paid off. He made a great small group of friends whom he still sees even today, so those self-goals are terrific. You have to make your own way at times, and this was one of those times. Brenden would also go on to join the TV news crew at this school, and that was where he decided to become a broadcast journalist. He was awesome behind the news desk, he had a great speaking voice, and he seemed to be the right fit for the news desk. Brenden would say to me, people recognize me now because they see me every morning! I really was happy for him, but behind the scenes, there were educational issues, not initially, but eventually, they became front and center. Four years went pretty fast, and there were many, many great teachers and paraprofessionals who really cared about Brenden and went the extra mile. You will read about them, and we will never forget them. Miracles were around us, and again, we were grateful. Unfortunately, there were things that had to be negotiated, and some things were not negotiable.

CHAPTER 19

COMPLAINTS I MADE A FEW

That summer, before high school started at an IEP meeting in the spring, it was recommended that Brenden should have ESY (extended school year) services by the team. For social skills, we discussed a program called Broadcast Journalism Academy being offered at the CCIU. This coincided with the goal on his IEP that he function as a part of a group and interact as a member of the group. I had attempted to register for this class online, but when I did, they requested payment. So, of course, since the school was paying for the class, I assumed they would just finish the registration. Under the regulations for ESY, the district as the public agency must ensure that the program is available, only if the IEP team determines this on an individual basis. This course had been cancelled. However, no one let us know from the district. Brenden was to also receive thirty minutes a week for speech to address conversational skills. Brenden's name was put on the list initially but somehow removed on the final list. So I wrote my complaint to the Department Of Education.

Amusing to me at the time were the answers given to the investigator assigned. The Director actually said that all I had to do when registering was click check as the method of payment, and the cost would have been billed back to the district. Even if I had known that, the class was cancelled, so either way, Brenden wasn't going. Wait, there is more. In reference to the speech services, she stated she had no idea of the omission until I filed the complaint. The speech services were able to be provided. However, the social skills program could not be. Therefore, we were rewarded compensatory services. Because the district named the program, they were held accountable for providing that particular class. But, honestly, although perhaps a victory, it really didn't give Brenden a ESY program. I was able to negotiate an alternative training, but honestly, so much time was wasted by the director of Special Education. She attempted to file for mediation and also for reconsideration. It was mid-October now, so I am sure you get my point. Everything set up in April to benefit Brenden turned into a six-month ordeal. Was it worth it? In fact, it was because the program we got would benefit Brenden in the future when he would learn how to use an iPad to make himself even more independent. There was a place called Springboard, and they offered a variety of courses related to video production, but we didn't choose that. We chose the lessons about managing an iPad, and that was well worth the trip and the compensation. Sometimes, although the road seems long and you are weary, remember it is all worth it. Brenden received twenty-two and a half hours of instruction on the device that would be his future. In the words of the Stones, "You can't always get what you want, but sometimes, you get what you need."

Brenden had received an iPad to use in classes. The idea behind that came from our great visual team support. It was trialed in several classes, and all teachers who were in the trial supported the use of the device for Brenden. However, in Spanish, there was a struggle, especially with processing a foreign language. Brenden wanted to try to record the classes or lectures, so he could use it to listen back to, as she spoke only Spanish, and this was Spanish 1. He didn't want a scribe or a notetaker in the class. He needed to become more independent. He was thinking college, and since he did not want a notetaker and he couldn't use his voice-recognition software during class, taping was the viable solution. The iPad had many apps to do so. One, for example, is AudioNote and SoundNote. Most of the teachers were on board with this, except for one—the one teacher who stated in her syllabus, "Under no circumstances will a student have permission to use a cell phone or recording device in my class." At the IEP meeting, I discussed the issue with her and tried to explain how

Brenden felt and that he was having trouble keeping up and completing assignments later. She told me, "My class is a scary place." I replied that I understood that because he was scared to death to go into her class. Brenden also had a reader for this class (someone to read the test questions in Spanish), but she felt that this would infringe upon the other students taking the test because they would hear the reader. She said later when we discussed the role of the reader that I had said translator. Perhaps, I may have said that I am not sure, but anything was possible. I am pretty sure I made many mistakes. I also asked where the curriculum was for this course, since I saw none other than what this teacher had on her syllabus. According to the assistant superintendent, there was no board approved curriculum for Spanish 1, only board-approved text materials. I thought, *No curriculum?* What standards were these, allowing a teacher make her own guidelines to what should be taught? I met with the assistant superintendent. She asked about the purpose of taping classes. When I attempted to explain that he was trying to have access to the lecture so he could later complete assignments, she insisted there would be other ways to do so. She referenced the textbook, and because of its age, there was no online version. Perhaps they could find an updated version. I was beyond wondering why all the exhausting effort was being made to hinder this taping of lectures. All he wanted was to be independent and succeed. I tried to share samples of Brenden's work from class and to discuss the difficulties. However, she made sure she told me she held the teacher in high regard and that the meeting was over. I knew as I walked out of that room, this was again going to be a ridiculous time-consuming endeavor. I also knew that Brenden was slowly becoming so anxiety ridden. He now had hives all over him one morning. He was becoming undone. I had to rescue him from this, because the worst days were to come. Soon, he would be in the abyss.

Using audio recording is a common accommodation that is widely used because it helps kids that have writing and processing problems, such as Brenden. It does not violate anyone's confidentiality. Neither FERPA (Family Educational Privacy Act) nor any other state law protects information that is openly shared in a public school classroom. It is in fact a right of a child with a disability to access their educational needs. After checking legally, the school did in fact say that taping would be allowed. However, one of the first things the teacher did was request a meeting with the department heads, the union, and an attorney. She then went further to write down what she thought should be included in the policy for recording lectures. I learned she requested that he could record, but it would be maintained by the school, that it only be used when necessary and that it be done on a cassette tape, never to leave the building. If you're laughing at this time, I completely understand. My question was, what in the world was she afraid of? The best part was she also stated if the recording did go home, the teacher and parent must sign a contract that the material would only be used for the student and not be shared with nondistrict parties. Specific consequences were to be administered if in violation of this agreement. Sure, how about felony charges? We literally were feeling a sense of desperation, like we were committing an unlawful act. A month of this, why would the district entertain her? This was becoming all about this teacher being unable to accept supporting a student. We were being reasonable when asking to tape a lecture, so it would allow for some repair to Brenden's inability to follow the lecture in a foreign language class.

It was mid-October now, and Brenden needed counseling. The teacher had no idea of how to allow a student who didn't learn like others survive in her class. I remember the back to school night when I went to her class, and I had heard things about her teaching style, heard she was tough on the kids, but I was always a person who wouldn't judge until I knew for myself. When I entered her class, the chairs were set up in a circle, and she stood in the middle, like a stage, like a performance would be. She began to greet us in Spanish. Well, I could handle that, and other parents giggled and thought it was charming. But it, then, continued. I am pretty sure most people in the room had no idea what she was saying. I sure didn't. Many parents got up and left. Some mumbled under their breath. I stayed because I needed to know what we would be up against. She finally started to speak English and told us of her background, which she then described herself as in the past being in the US Army and the

US Department of Justice. She said she was a strong believer in structure in the classroom. That seemed okay with me. Our family was a military family. I understood she wanted respect, high expectations, and dedication. Did you ever hear about first impressions? Well, they really do mean a lot. Dismally, she, in fact, just wanted things to be done her way. For example, when learning vocabulary, Brenden wanted to use a flash card app, with the Spanish word on one side and the English word on another side. She said no, she wanted him to draw the picture, an absolutely frustrating assignment. He needed to use his voice recognition for writing assignments, but she did not allow this and later admitted that she had no idea how that could work. Brenden was removed from the class to take a test, because he had a reader. She stated that it disrupted the other students in the class, and when she went around the room to check for homework assignments, she didn't check his but assumed he would just e-mail to her.

I had pleaded with her to at least put the directions for assignments in English. This finally did happen but only after three weeks of asking. I totally didn't understand. If he couldn't understand the directions, how would he be able to do the assignment? One particular assignment was to write twenty-four vocabulary words three times each. He asked if he could make flash cards instead as writing was extremely difficult. She agreed but later told him he would lose fifteen points because he did not do the assignment correctly. When he had to write in her class, he was denied to use his voice-recognition software, and she referred to him as a disruption (Brenden speaking while others are thinking and writing). She could not figure out how to move him to another area so he could speak and not be that disturbing figure she referenced, her choice of words always demeaning. She would say that his homework didn't capture the spirit of the homework. Her grades for his homework were 0/15 for not following directions. She would ask the autistic support teachers for help or tell them they weren't helping her or him properly. In fact, she did admit she had no training in teaching students who were on the spectrum. She felt I was negative when I e-mailed her and did not give her any concrete feedback. I would have if she had only asked. I tried to offer suggestions, and Brenden did as well. I could have tried harder, I suppose. I don't know. I thought I was. She really made it all about her needs and mostly just failed Brenden as a student in her class. Complaints this teacher made were the priority, not the educational needs of the student.

With the delay of the taping accommodation, Brenden started to feel like he couldn't keep up. He was having trouble sleeping. He was lost and starting to panic. He called himself a loser. He started to regress and have meltdowns at home, followed by obsessive things like washing his hands and feet over and over. I had to get him out of that class . . . and that's exactly what I did but not before her ultimate attack occurred.

CHAPTER 20

OFFICE OF CIVIL RIGHTS

The Office of Civil Rights prohibits discrimination on the basis of race, color, national origin, sex, disability, and age in programs or activities that receive federal financial assistance from the Department of Education. In Title II of the Americans with Disabilities Act of 1990 and section 504 of the Rehabilitation Act of 1973, discrimination on the basis of disability by public entities, whether or not they receive federal financial assistance, is prohibited. This extends to all state education agencies, elementary and secondary school systems, colleges and universities, libraries, and museums, to name a few. Couple of things time is a factor because your complaint must be filed within 180 calendar days of the alleged discrimination. You absolutely can use the procedural safeguards, as you are entitled to do. However, I had been down that road, and this was something that I had researched because of all the intimidation tactics this teacher was using, but the final blow was the day that Brenden came home to show me two index cards. One had the word *Hall* on it; the other an abbreviation *BR*, which meant *bathroom*. Brenden explained that this had been handed to him by the paraprofessional in the room so that he could hold these up in the air if he needed to take a visual break or use the bathroom. I couldn't even believe my eyes as my son handed me these cards. He was in shock. I was told after asking three times why she humiliated him like this, that the cards were merely indicator cards. This, in her mind, gave him the opportunity to excuse himself without attention being drawn. Really? In no other class were there issues about going to the rest room or taking a visual break. Brenden had on his IEP a statement that he could use a permanent pass to use the bathroom. The school had required that you take your agenda to the bathroom as your pass. Brenden struggled with that because he had nowhere to put it, so he had a pass to keep in his pocket. This they countered allowed him to use the bathroom anytime he wanted. That was not true. He still had to request to go, just like everyone else. He just did not need to take a book to the bathroom. The teacher responded that she did this so he did not have to be a distraction to the other students in the class or an unnecessary delay for Brenden. Here is Brenden's version of the story. He tells it the best, as it is unparalleled to anything I could ever say about this incident.

Brenden's Landscape

Dear Office of Civil Rights,

My name is Brenden Curry. I am in tenth grade. I am fifteen years old, and I have high-functioning autism. Throughout my life, I've worked hard to achieve many great things. I've worked hard to communicate, becoming more social and including myself with my peers, and preparing for college transition.

I am writing this letter to address the horrendous events in Spanish 1 class. She taught her class with an iron fist mentality with no mercy. Every day, I was scared to go to her class because she taught her class speaking in 99.9 percent Spanish. With my autism, this is an issue when it comes to processing the information. I've always had problems processing information, and she wouldn't allow any former translator or translation to English. She never allowed any English spoken in her class. I couldn't understand the tasks or anything she wanted the class including me to do.

On my IEP (Individual Education Plan), I am allowed to use assistive technology. The assistive technology is a seventeen-inch Dell Vostro 1720 laptop and an Apple iPad 2. The software I primarily use for school is Adobe Acrobat to view my schoolwork in PDF format and Dragon NaturallySpeaking for writing essays. On my iPad 2, the apps I use are Goodreader and iAnnotate for viewing PDF files, iBooks for reading books, Pages for writing prompts and essays, Keynote for viewing PowerPoints. They were two apps I use on my iPad that she denied the use of. These apps are Flashcards and iTranslate and iSpeak Spanish for translating. As I mentioned earlier, she denied the use of translating, but she also denied me the use of using my flash card app for creating flash cards. She believes that having translation does not make the student learn the Spanish language. She also believes that it's cheating to use translation to English. With my processing difficulties, having a translator or the use of my translating apps would have helped me understand Spanish better, but with her denial and noncooperation, I struggled, and I felt behind. I feel that she violated my IEP.

I did end up using the flash card app for some vocabulary, but I didn't get credit for the assignment. I used that app to reduce the frustration I was experiencing when it came to these types of assignments she would assign. When she assigned us to "write the Spanish word three times and the English word once," I decided to make flash cards of those words to reduce the frustration for me. I was basically helping myself. When I showed it to her, she asked me, "Bernardo (my name for Spanish class), where is your homework?" I said, "It's in the flash card app on my iPad." Then I show it to her, and she said, "I'm not going to give you credit for that." I did the same assignment as the thirty other kids in that class, but she didn't give me credit for the assignment. Instead, I got a zero. This made me feel angry because I used my accommodations for assignments without getting credit.

Handing in assignments was very confusing. In all classes that involved my laptop, I would usually e-mail or print the assignment for my teachers to grade. In Spanish, the turning in of assignments was very off and on and with lots of changes. This means that she wants me to e-mail the assignment but then changes her mind, and she would want me hand in the assignment printed from my laptop. She also said that she will give me feedback on how I did. Her feedback was the most ridiculous and embarrassing I've ever read. She'll type things like "Bernardo, please make this text in purple font color so I can see that you corrected your work" for homework and daily question responses or "Bernardo, please remember to write, 'Mi nombre es Bernardo Curry. Mi maestra es _____. La clase de Español 1. Hoy es 20 de septiembre" for Collins writing prompts.

The homework was written in Spanish under "La tarea de hoy," meaning "today's homework," and the assignment was even written in Spanish. On her homework, there were no or a few English translations. When homework was first assigned during the first two weeks of school, I could not understand what she wanted me to complete. The directions on the homework were also in Spanish. I couldn't even understand the directions printed on the worksheet to complete. Copying down the homework in my iPad calendar app was also difficult and confusing. I had a hard time typing on my iPad with the Spanish keyboard on the screen. I also had trouble with the daily "Pregunta del día," meaning "question of the day." The question of the day was also written in Spanish, and there were multiple occasions where I could not answer the question of the day. Most of the time, I would just write one word in Spanish and even just write the answer in English.

One day, my paraprofessional gave me these two index cards. One set *BR* for *bathroom* while the other one said *Hall* for breaks. I was shocked when I was given these cards and felt humiliated. When this event occurred, I also felt that my dignity, honor, vigor, morale, and especially respect from others had been taken away from me. I felt like I was treated like a lower-functioning student, and I also felt that she took advantage of me. I was not going to raise them up in the middle of class and embarrass myself. There were a handful of freshmen, plus three to four sophomores and two juniors in that class. As a sophomore, I'm a role model for the freshmen, and I want to impress the upperclassmen such as those two juniors. I wanted respect from everyone, and by raising index cards that say either *BR* or *Hall* will make them think negatively about me. As I discussed about me working on my social skills, I want to be accepted by the typical student body, and me raising those two cards would just derail the social progress I've made the last two to three years.

My ultimate goal is to go to college. I want to have a career in journalism and broadcasting. My mother believes that I have potential and that I could be successful despite my disabilities and adversities. When I was doing course selection, I kept hearing that colleges want at least two years of language. My father, Dennis Curry, told me that I should take Spanish because Spanish would be more beneficial than French, Italian, and German. My mother agreed that I should also take Spanish because it's the easiest out of the four languages offered at High School. With my decision to drop Spanish due to mental health issues such as anxiety, I feel like that my chances of getting into college are being jeopardized.

I want to make something of myself, and college is going to be my ticket to success. I want to live the life of a typical American man who has a job, car, house, friends, and family that will love and cherish him. I want to eventually live independently with a job and a family. I feel that a college degree will take me to the promised land of normalcy. I worked hard throughout my life, and I've experienced the good and worst of times. Most of my early life, I've experienced hardships. One of my hardships was communicating. When I was in first grade, I couldn't speak English, because of my autism and my inability to express myself. I've worked hard throughout my elementary years, and I've made significant progress. When I was in Spanish experiencing this, I felt like I was in kindergarten and first grade all over again. I've also got anxiety from her class, and the anxiety got so bad that I got hives throughout my body and had to see a psychologist, and I still do.

Thank you for your consideration and interests in my case. I hope for the best, and I also hope that this letter will influence your decision. May God bless you all as the OCR makes their decision on my case.

What I liked about filing with OCR was that they called and spoke with you directly. They asked you to clarify your statements and make sure you were clear in the allegations. Basically, they were neutral, and that is how you get to the bottom of things and to the truth. I remember the attorney asking me specifically what did I want to see as an outcome. All I wanted was educational compensation for Brenden. He needed this language class to possibly be admitted into college. Was I angry about the situation? Was I feeling horrible that Brenden had to endure that treatment? I was, but again eye on the prize. The district decided to agree to voluntary resolution, and I think they did because the OCR looks at what could be the solution and how the person voicing the complaint can become whole. There was no reason to have Brenden hold cards up to get what he needed. He was able to do so on his own. Why did she have to do this? There was no reason for the teacher to be concerned about her own rights because a student wanted to tape a lecture, an allowable accommodation. Again, this took months. Brenden was in school but just not in that Spanish class.

However, before he entered eleventh grade, things came together. In the OCR drafted agreement, the words were stated, *"Requesting and granting of permission to the student to use the bathroom will be done in the same manner for him as the nondisabled students."* This liberated Brenden. He felt vindication. He did not then or now need any assistance to use the bathroom. I never will forget his statements to me at that time when he said, "I feel like I am going to die." There were other good results that evolved as well. The following was required of the district:

    a)   The district is obligated to provide services to qualified students with disabilities consistent with Section 504's regulations at 34 CFR 104, et seq, which includes a statement that implementation of an IEP developed under the Individuals with Disabilities Education Act is one means of meeting those standards.

    b)   All provisions of a student's IEP must be promptly and fully implemented.

c) Any failure to implement a student's IEP is a form of disability discrimination.

d) Treating a student with disabilities different than students without disabilities is a form of disability discrimination, unless the different treatment is necessary to provide the student with a free and appropriate public education.

Brenden continued in counseling but was allowing himself to let go and move on with his goals of attending college. We also got to discuss educational loss, in which our private psychologist wrote a magnificent letter to outline his direct loss of learning, his loss of credit and opportunity for his future. She also attended the IEP meeting where I was attempting to get educational compensation for Brenden. I was so touched by her dedication and commitment. I think I would be remiss here if I did not speak of how single-handedly this psychologist restored my son when I handed him to her broken and fragmented. There is no reason to not seek this outside resource help for your child, if warranted. It is hard for a parent not to be emotionally attached with all aspects of their child's life. There are times that others may be able to help where you have perhaps failed or in this case couldn't handle it alone.

There was also a second look at taping of lectures and since the policy had been instituted already with other staff at the school, there was much success to talk about. I appreciated the effort the current Director of Special Education had given on this issue, in creating the taping policy, it was no small feat. Brenden had already completed and taped lectures in five health classes, and no one objected. He did not receive compensatory education in Spanish. I just couldn't prove there was a failure to provide FAPE (Fair and Appropriate Education) for regular education, but was able to start eleventh grade with a tutor to prepare him to again take Spanish 1. He successfully completed Spanish 2 in his senior year. Great teacher by the way. She was warm, her room was inviting, and she saw in Brenden what he could accomplish with her help. It was like night and day for him, but he tackled the challenge, and success was all he saw.

When I requested Brenden's complete educational records, which is your right to do by the way, I found an e-mail the first Spanish teacher had written, and she said that there needed to be a standard set, one rule for all situations. "Since Brenden was a black-and-white processor, then we should make his environment as black/white as we possibly can, right?" "Preferences don't really play out in a classroom too well for a teacher with twenty-eight kids." Black-and-white thinker she says; that couldn't be farther from the truth. Brenden is the most engaging and respectful person I know. She had no idea of what he had accomplished since he was six years old. His work ethic and strong desire to improve never entered her mind. Brenden had a beautiful mind. All he wanted to do was to access his tools in her classroom so he could learn, so he could go to college. She just did not understand how to teach someone who learned differently. She was rigid. She did not think out of the box. She was not going to negotiate. First impressions do mean a lot, and she did not disappoint.

CHAPTER 21

CONGLOMERATION

The best advice I could ever possibly give any parent is when you feel you cannot figure out what in the world is going on in your child's head, seek professional help. Not that you cannot get inside your child's head; it is just others can do that without freaking out. They are not emotionally tied in. They can be that third party who doesn't judge you or want to change you. They are there to help. We had the best. She helped Brenden reflect on things, especially after a rough day, which in his mind was pretty constant. As a parent, you are at times completely overwhelmed, and functioning as a counselor is not feasible. At times, she was also a resource and comfort to me. Often when a tense or problematic situation would come up, we could meet and have a session together. I really do not know what I would have done without her wisdom and support. Weekly sessions seemed to keep things running smoothly. She was part of our village.

Private counseling enabled Brenden to do some pretty difficult things, and best of all, the support allowed him to be a risk-taker, someone who could continue to defy the odds. He wanted to drive. At seventeen, he took the permit test and failed. He never went back. But when he turned eighteen, he set a goal to get that permit after his first year in college, which was a rough one, but that is not my story to tell. In thinking about the test, he was so anxious, but he prepared, and we went. I remember during the test the computer stopped working, and he was interrupted twice. I thought this is going to shake him, but he even goes over to the examiner and asks if the test can be read to him, and *he aces the test*! As he walked toward me, he was slightly smiling, and I suppose a little in shock of what just transpired. As we sat and waited for assistance to actually get that permit, we met a father and his son waiting to renew his permit, for the third time. The father stated that his son was now nineteen years old, and I thought, *Well, that is kind of our story.* However, as I looked over at the young man, he seemed unable to converse, no eye contact. I looked over at Brenden. I was so grateful he had that ability and he could be social. As we left the DMV, Brenden was jumping for joy literally! Another hurdle to cross off the list of goals completed. Now the driving part . . .

The first time out was chaotic to say the least. Just using the gas, then the brake was a challenge, and of course, his processing was slow. We were in a parking lot alone, but as soon as someone entered the lot, he panicked, stepping on the gas instead of the brake. My nerves! I thought, *I may not be capable of teaching him how to drive. Am I not saying the correct things?* But we get through it, and every day, he practices turns, pulling into parking spots and backing out. All was good except I feel like every day I am saying the same things as well. It isn't clicking. So we are going to be in the parking lot a little while until he is ready to get onto the road. This is no different than any other thing he had to learn, like walking. A good friend of mine, Havi, told me driving is a skill to master, give it time. This is how things work and are managed in his world, but it can wear him down, because everything is a challenge, one right after another. One day, he was so undone, he told me I was criticizing him. I felt like it was feedback on driving. I mean, was I just to say nothing? I was hurt, but later that day, I understood and accepted how he felt. The very next time we went driving, I said, "Let's get out of this parking lot and hit the back roads." He did just that and did great, went out, and turned left into traffic. All the impatient drivers behind him beeping and all, he was so happy. I told him, "Ignore the beepers, Brenden. You are *driving*!" In trying not to overwhelm him, I wasn't believing in him, I suppose. We were in parking lots for two weeks;

he needed to move on. I had to give him the courage I had to show him he could do this, and he handled it just fine.

Of course, out in the rural roads, you encounter some unusual things, and we had a bunch of geese crossing the road. It appeared, Brenden was not going to stop, and I had to scream, "*Stop!*" This is so funny now, but what are the chances of geese crossing? I had to ask him what he intended to do. He said, "I really didn't know what to do." FYI, no geese were harmed in the making of a new PA driver! He nailed the test and the parallel parking. He still is nervous about driving alone in the car, but this is just another challenge, a hurdle, and one day, he will drive without a passenger. I said, "Driving here to there is fine and something you have to do daily. Your success will be found on easy street."

So remember the joy and great teachers that abetted Brenden in high school. I never mentioned them. Like I said, I would. All I wrote about was the struggle. My advice is find the joy and celebrate that no matter how tough things can get. I am not saying we did not do that, but I can reflect now that time passed by so quickly. I may have been neglecting the joy factor.

Brenden often talked about his journalism teacher Mr. Gregory. He was his mentor, but he also gave Brenden great confidence by allowing him to showcase his ability to write. Brenden was on the school newspaper for years, as the sports writer. He loved sports, and he was really talented at capturing the story within the story. Honestly, this man has never been replaced in Brenden's life. That's how significant of a person he was. When someone helps you build a foundation upon which you can build your future, it means the world to you. Brenden's potential was there untapped and then came opportunity. Mr. Gregory recommended him for the job of writing for EasternPAFootball. This online publication covered all the high school football games, and it was his first attempt at writing sports articles for something other than the school newspaper. Brenden would cover his home team's football games in the press box, while his teacher was the announcer for the games. He really covered the game, including the spirit of the game, by digging deep to showcase the players, even though the team had many losses. He would use his iPad and record the after game interviews. It was so helpful for him, and he could then go home after the game and put his article together. I volunteered to be his editor, so I would stay up late with him and really just admire his work.

I made sure that in the last teacher conference, I got to thank Mr. Gregory for all he had done for Brenden. I wanted him to know how much he meant to him, and because he was that mentor, Brenden had been able to find what motivated him. He still talks about this teacher till this day, and I will be forever grateful for his kindness and passion for journalism. He truly inspired Brenden to be someone.

Diane Mascitelli, she was the materials specialist at the school. She was responsible for making things readable for Brenden. In other words, she was the production person that enlarged things for him and turned them into PDF versions so that he could read them digitally. She sent an e-mail to the vision support staff and the subject was "Shakespeare—to have blue illustrations or not to have blue illustrations that is the question." She was referring to when she took the book apart to scan it and was asking if she could leave the blue illustrations in place. She stated, *I was thinking it would be nice for him to get close to the book experience but only if it is correct for him.* All I can say and did say at the time was, "Wow!" She was an amazing person to care that he have a real book experience, such human kindness, such empathy for what she thought he might be missing. I also asked to meet her and thank her for thinking of Brenden as more than the visually impaired kid whom she prepared documents for. She understood that reading digitally wasn't wonderful for him, and she tried to make things better. She was awesome and magnificent.

The Holiday Holla was an annual talent show that was held, and Brenden could sing. He had participated in a talent show in middle school. He sang a Johnny Cash's song "Ring of Fire." He did great. I remember we borrowed our old neighbors guitar because he was feeling a bit awkward about just standing there singing. He couldn't play, but who knew that! In high school, he decided to participate in their annual event at Christmastime. You had to audition for the Holla, and he was nervous, but he sang "I've Got the World on a String" by Michael Bublé. He really loved to sing his songs, and it was a perfect fit for him. He really brought down the house. We got to see the dress rehearsal and a lot of parents were there, and he did just great. He participated every year after that and looked forward to it as well. Besides being an announcer for the daily school news, this was something that gave him confidence and allowed him to be social. He was a face of the morning news whom other students recognized. He coined the phrase "It's Hoagie Day!" on the morning announcements. He had the support of many friends and others who were in the competition, and in later years, he was able to perform a duo with a friend.

Brenden also was chosen for several awards and scholarships as a senior. Members of the faculty at the school nominated him for student of the month for the local Lions Club. He was recognized for his efforts in academics, service to the school and community, and leadership. It was thrilling for him, as it was with all of us. We attended a dinner that included the awards being given to each student. He got his name up in lights at the high school. We absolutely went over to capture that picture!

At the end of his high school years, there were scholarships and awards. He was chosen to receive the principal's award. Brenden did not know he was receiving the award but was asked to have a speech ready. All we heard beforehand was that he would be extremely happy. Everyone we saw on the way in was elated to say they couldn't wait. We were like, "Wow, okay!" But his speech, Brenden wanted to say so much, and when he spoke, I was happy for him. I cried, and my daughter Emily held my hand. It was the highest honor to receive this award, to be recognized in the totality of your class for excellence. They also asked if you wanted to buy a memorial brick to line the entrance to the Stadium. I said that we didn't need a brick, because Brenden was made of stone and perhaps just kissed the Blarney Stone, indeed! Here is what Brenden said on that great day:

> Going into my freshman year, I was a quiet
> person who had a rolling suitcase with my laptop
> and school supplies in it. I was adjusting to using
> a laptop for viewing my schoolwork. I was also

very motivated to begin my high school years. I can remember saying to my mother that "My future begins when I go to high school."

I also had very few friends going into my freshman year. I was socially awkward due to my autism. I would play musical chairs just to find the lunch table I feel comfortable with. I knew that I wanted to be social and to include myself in activities. I also realized that I needed to focus my high school years by preparing for a career in broadcasting and journalism. I got involved with the TV studio, which boosted my self-confidence. This led me to become social with everyone at school. I developed many relationships with people here due to my exposure on the TV every morning. Many people admired me for disclosing my autism on live TV for Autism Awareness Month that year.

I also got involved with the Holiday Holla by showcasing my singing talent. My involvement in the school newspaper, *The Devil's Herald*, also gave me many memories. I interviewed many people from all walks of the school community for my articles and found the stories within the stories through my print. My hard work and contributions to the school newspaper led me to earning a huge opportunity for me not to lose. I obtained an internship with EasternPAFootball. com as a reporter covering High School football games, where I wrote game reports, interviews, along with statistics. Over the two seasons, they only won two games. However, I used this experience of covering a team who came short of victories as a lesson for me as a sports journalist.

I'm grateful for being given a chance to do such a fun and challenging internship as a high school student. My contributions also led me to several honors this school year that I never expected. I was named the Lions Club senior of the month in November. I realized why I was nominated because of a quote The principal told me. After he read me the letter, he then told me of how much of an impact I made on the school community by stepping up to the plate where others decided to sit on the bleachers. I was also voted by my peers for having the most school spirit. At first, I thought that school spirit meant run around the school wearing the colors and cheering! I found that people voted for me because of my journalism and how I covered the athletic teams. I am excited for what lies ahead of me as I set sail to become a Millersville Marauder next fall. These last four years have built my foundation to become college bound and have a career in broadcasting and journalism.

Brenden was also the recipient of some scholarships as well, and then he applied for others to help fund his college costs. You really have to work at getting the scholarships. It is a continued effort of writing and rewriting essays. It did help him, and we never were able to save any money toward funding that future, and as my sister always said, "Even if you did, it wouldn't be enough!" Here is an article he wrote as a staff writer while in school—pretty spot-on, honest, and full of insight as only he could deliver!

A Student's Insights on Autism

Brenden Curry
Staff Writer

In math class, probability is one of the many mathematical concepts taught to students.

According to Dictionary.com, it is "a strong likelihood or chance of something." Have you ever dealt with a probability that has the odds of 1 in 88? Would this ratio make an event more likely to occur or not likely to happen? If you answered likely, then you're correct.

The ratio 1 in 88 is the new statistic for a child being diagnosed with autism.

Autism is a neurological disorder that affects a person's communication and social skills. According to the Centers for Disease Control and Prevention, there are three criteria with six or more items needing to be present, to diagnose autism or autism spectrum disorder.

The first item is social interaction. This includes eye contact, failure to develop peer relationships, and the inability to read and express emotions.

The second deficit is communication. A child may have language, but he/she can lose it, sustaining conversations with peers and not having the ability to initiate conversation. There could also be a lack of use of imagination.

The final category is repetitive behaviors. Preoccupation with certain interests and repetitive behaviors such as the flapping of the hands or snapping fingers and inflexibility with routine changes are examples.

Many people take having the ability to communicate for granted. There are people in this world that will never speak.

When it comes to social interaction. I used to be very isolated. Many of you see *me as a friendly, outgoing person, but I was not that person ten years ago.*

I can remember being frustrated at school because I couldn't express myself or communicate my needs.

Having conversations with people was a challenge for me because I didn't know what to say to them or what to talk about. I had minimal eye contact with the person I was conversing with.

I was in my own little world mentally where I was isolated from the outside world.

Communication was my biggest problem. It is very frustrating when you can't express yourself and tell people what you need or what you want to say. I had trouble with words and turning words into sentences.

With a deficit in verbal communication, learning sign language was the way to go. After I started to sign, my mother knew how important speech and language therapy would be. I had to go to speech therapy for five days a week when I was younger.

Many people take having the ability to communicate for granted. There are people in this world who will never speak in their lifetime or have trouble with finding words that relate to their specific needs.

With new technologies being invented every day, nonverbal autistic children now have hope to learn how to speak. Learning and having the ability to communicate will make a person feel less frustrated.

Surprisingly, I did have repetitive behaviors. Ten years ago, I wasn't as open as I am now. I did have preoccupations with Thomas the Tank Engine, SpongeBob SquarePants, *and sports. I was obsessed with* Thomas the Tank Engine *because playing with those wooden trains made me feel calm, and I knew that I was organized.*

Even though I've outgrown *Thomas the Tank Engine*, I still use Sir Topham Hatt's "confusion and delay" quote.

Out of those three preoccupations, sports have stuck with me the most. I do relate almost everything to sports. Sports have made me feel included with my peers and a good conversation starter.

Sports is an obsession that will never go away, and my future will involve my passion for sports as a journalist or broadcaster.

Like all human beings, autistic people want to be included with their typical peers. People need to accept the fact that autistic *people function differently, but they are also human. They want to try and fit in and be accepted by everyone.*

Even though many people accept me for who I am, I'm still trying to fit in. Many people participate in sports, band/choir, school play, and other extracurricular activities. When people are involved in activities like sports, they feel that they fit in with their peers. I've found the way to be accepted the hard way.

In order for me to fit in, I played musical chairs at lunch just to find the table I felt comfortable with.

Reading the morning announcements and singing in the Holiday Holla have given me the opportunity to show my talents to the student body.

I've received respect from others by my kindness, honesty, and motivation to be successful.

Many people can spread awareness about autism, but what matters most is acceptance. Accepting someone who is different can make every-

one involved become more peaceful, loving, caring, and friendly.

As sportswriter and author Mitch Albom's old college professor Morrie Schwartz from *Tuesdays with Morrie* always said, "The culture we have does not make people feel good about themselves. And you have to be strong enough to say if the culture doesn't work, don't buy it."

What Morrie said is worth following; I try to live this aphorism every day.

CHAPTER 22

PREPARING FOR COLLEGE 101

So Brenden was going to college, but honestly, I was freaking out. How could I just send him off? I mean what was I thinking? He was hardly prepared for college life! Nah! Just kidding. There are programs for that. Not that it covers everything, but it is like boot camp for first-time moms and gives you some perspective. So instead of ESY for other things, we chose to ask for a program called ASPIRE. It was a summer program on the campus of West Chester University that ran for a week. It was to mimic a typical day in the life of a college student. They offered college-based classes and one credit. It was on the campus of a university but without massive amounts of people. This was offered through the Chester County IU, and I have to say they have always been such a resource to us, to Brenden.

When we got there, he was already assigned a roommate, and that was interesting. Let's just say that when we got to the room, it was locked. The other boy and his family were in there, and they wouldn't open the door. When they did let us in, he had already decided he was on the side of the room with the only TV cable, and he did not have a TV, nor did he want one on his side of the room. He then proceeded to tell us that he wanted to find out if he could burn incense in the room, and he had other ideas. So Brenden and I hit the lobby to see about changing roommates. They were familiar with our new friend. He was a frequent guest. So they were able to come up and suggest that he negotiate changing beds so that everyone had what they needed and also explained that burning anything would not be following the rules. Success, all was well. We switched things up, then found we had no cable for the TV! This is what husbands are for, so we sent Dennis, AKA the husband, out for the cable. Can you feel my anxiety and my helicopter parenting? *Yes!* But after that, it was okay. They had TSS workers in the building, and they would be there all throughout. Great, great idea and program. They had the bathroom that was down the hall. There was no WIFI in the building, and I was also thinking, *This is not a fit for him for college hands down,* although technically, he needed to have WIFI, because he was technology dependent. Such is life. We move on right?

They offered a college course called Society and Social Reasoning, along with Emotional Regulation and Stress Reduction. They did a review of technology with each student, transportation and safety, and career coursework planning. Brenden had leisure time and really enjoyed the independence about that. He was able to be in a city and function by himself but also had the backup of support. I was on the other hand a nervous wreck! Walking away for the very first time was the ultimate challenge for me! I was on the phone to my dear friend Helena, and she kept me together. The best part it was close, so I was thirty minutes tops. It was a success. It was needed. It was a great learning curve. Nothing can prepare you for this transition, but it really became a great convenience to what was next. I have to say that everything is difficult to get through, but why not take the chance! Everyone makes mistakes, but you learn and move on. Everything is possible if you just believe! Look for these types of programs. Search Speak Up. It is important. Sometimes, it is not all or nothing but what is in between. Search for the in-between.

Now with Brenden graduating from college this year, I find that things are as they should be. He can write about college. That's an entire book on its own! There are still some moments that I hold my breath, and other moments, I can breathe normally. It has been a journey, and I believe everything for a reason. I have great hopes for Brenden's bright future and cannot wait to see all he will accomplish. When I asked him if he wanted to recover from autism, he stated he liked who he was. I'd have to agree.

My mom had been a writer. She had that gift. She inspired this book. She always was there for me. Brenden loved her so. She was his *au pair*. She had a way with words. In her last written words to me, she said, "Being of simple mind, taking one day at a time, and hoping for the best, but a great saying, 'Don't think about it. Just do it!' I will say I have five children, Kate being one specially loved. It is hard to spread it around, but you do your best. This may not be acceptable to all children, but try it. It is one tough job, parenting. You will do what your own mother taught you if you watched her and remember what sacrifices were made without much thought for herself. Love and respect always—number one, no matter what. Think good thoughts. It will be your turn. Do your best." Love, Mom.

The movie *Pay It Forward* was a favorite of myself and my mom. In the movie, they refer to the fact that everybody is so used to things being bad and cannot believe they can change it. They become losers. She wrote quotes from the story in her writing book. Good words to live by.

"Protect them. See what they need. Listen to them. But it can change. Make another wish. Don't blow out the candle just yet."

"Life is a journey. Forgive yourself. Forgive others. A short journey, don't let it end, before you meet the challenge. You're down, and then you get up."

"You're constantly being tested. Make mistakes. Admit it. Then make life a little better. You can change everything! Laugh and cry, but go on. A little wisdom can be a bad thing, but it can be beneficial."

BIBLIOGRAPHY

"How to File a Discrimination Complaint with the Office for Civil Rights." Home, US Department of Education (ED), 17 Nov. 2017, www2.ed.gov/about/offices/list/ocr/docs/howto.html.

http://www.answers.com/Q/What_do_you_get_if_you_kiss_the_Blarney_Stone

"IDEA—The Individuals with Disabilities Education Act." Center for Parent Information and Resources, www.parentcenterhub.org/idea/.

"IDEA—The Individuals with Disabilities Education Act." Center for Parent Information and Resources, www.parentcenterhub.org/idea/.

"Insight Online." RNIB—Supporting People with Sight Loss, 7 Nov. 2016, www.rnib.org.uk/insight-online.

"Kidspiration—The Visual Way to Explore and Understand Words, Numbers and Concepts." Develop Elementary Reading Comprehension, Writing and Math Skills with Kidspiration®, www.inspiration.com/Kidspiration.

"Learn the Signs. Act Early." Centers for Disease Control and Prevention, Centers for Disease Control and Prevention, 14 Feb. 2018, www.cdc.gov/ncbddd/actearly/index.html.

Sniderman, Amy. "Abnormal Head Growth." Pediatrics in Review, American Academy of Pediatrics, 1 Sept. 2010, pedsinreview.aappublications.org/content/31/9/382?sso=1&sso_redirect_count=5&nfstatus=401&nftoken=00000000-0000-0000-0000-000000000000&nfstatusdescription=ERROR%3A+No+local+token.

"What Is Autism?" Autism Society, www.autism-society.org/what-is/.
http://www.answers.com/Q/What_do_you_get_if_you_kiss_the_
    Blarney_Stone

ABOUT THE AUTHOR

Kate Curry holds a degree in nursing and a PhD in persistence. She never gave up. Kate chose adoption, and that journey led her to becoming a mother. She had no clue her son Brenden would eventually be diagnosed with autism. The years ahead were filled with turmoil, yet the unimaginable happened. Her son will graduate in 2018 with a degree in digital journalism. Kate changed careers to work with children on the spectrum and found new perspective. Kate also volunteered for the CDC's Learn the Signs Act Early Campaign. She and Brenden took any opportunity to spread awareness. For the better part of her son's twelve years of education, she navigated and advocated to find an appropriate education. It took years trying to figure things out. There was failure and great success, and the chances taken tell the story.

You may encounter many defeats, but you must not be defeated. In fact, it may be necessary to encounter the defeats so you know who you are, what you can rise from, how you can still come out of it.
—Maya Angelou